BUILD YOUR FOUNDATION

Six Must-Have Beliefs for Constructing an Unshakable Christian Life

RICK RENNER

Build Your Foundation:
Six Must-Have Beliefs for Constructing an Unshakable Christian Life
ISBN: 9781680315806
Ebook 9781680315813
POD LP 9781680315820
POD HC 9781680315837
Copyright © 2021 by Rick Renner
8316 E. 73rd St.
Tulsa, OK 74133

Published by Harrison House
Shippensburg, PA 17257-2914
www.harrisonhouse.com

2 3 4 5 6 / 25 24 23 22 21

Editorial Consultants: Cynthia D. Hansen and Rebecca L. Gilbert
Text Design: Lisa Simpson, www.SimpsonProductions.net

DEDICATION

I dedicate this doctrinal "primer" to the Sunday school teachers who influenced my life as I was growing up in our home church. Under the leadership of our pastor, these dear believers faithfully taught me and others nearly all the fundamental principles that are covered in this book. Our church provided me with solid teaching on so many of the essential basics of God's Word, and for this I will be forever thankful. The doctrinal truths they poured into my young life contributed to the foundation for my life and ministry today.

CONTENTS

Acknowledgments

I want to acknowledge those who impacted my life with the solid teaching of the Bible early on. From my parents to my Sunday school teachers to my childhood pastor, I say thank you for imparting an unshakable conviction of the importance of God's Word into my life. Much of who I am and what I do today is a result of all those who laid the foundational truths of God's Word in my life when I was young. Over the years, there have also been others whose insights and teaching have deeply impacted me, and I am thankful to them as well for their vital role in my personal spiritual growth.

In this book, I cover the six "building blocks" that are essential for a person to have the kind of strong spiritual foundation that was established in my life in the early years. I am thankful that my friend, Keith Trump, a gifted scholar of the Greek New Testament, read this manuscript before it was sent to be printed and provided several valuable additions. I am thankful for his helpful recommendations. I am likewise thankful to Cindy Hansen and to my editorial team at RENNER Ministries for hovering over every word to make sure this book reflects what I want to convey to my readers.

For when for the time ye ought to be teachers,

ye have need that one teach you again

which be the first principles of the oracles of God;

and are become such as have need of milk,

and not of strong meat. For every one that useth milk

is unskilful in the word of righteousness:

for he is a babe. But strong meat belongeth to them

that are of full age, even those who by reason of use

have their senses exercised to discern both good and evil.

Therefore leaving the principles of the doctrine of Christ,

let us go on unto perfection; not laying again the foundation

of repentance from dead works, and of faith toward God,

of the doctrine of baptisms, and of laying on of hands,

and of resurrection of the dead, and of eternal judgment.

Hebrews 5:12 – 6:2

1

GROWING BEYOND THE ABCS OF THE CHRISTIAN FAITH

The ancient city of Ephesus was a place of great education and learning in ancient times. Situated right in the heart of the city was an amazing place called Philosophers' Square, crowned with the magnificent Library of Celsus, the third-largest library in the world at the time it was built in the year 110 AD. Appropriately called "the light of Asia," Ephesus attracted people from all over the continent who came to study and learn in this city and in this unique facility. The ruins still stand as a striking testimony to its former greatness.

For example, great arches still stand at one side of the Philosophers' Square through which people walked as they entered the Central Marketplace. Interestingly, too, there is some archeological evidence that suggests an open-air synagogue from the First Century formerly stood in its place.

Directly opposite the arches are steps leading up to what was once called the School of Tyrannus, where the apostle Paul taught New Testament doctrine to countless people for more than two years while he resided in Ephesus. Acts 19:9,10 tells us that he taught it every morning and afternoon to whomever had a heart to hear and understand — until, finally, the name of Jesus and the Gospel message was heard and known all over Asia.

Why would the apostle Paul commit to that kind of rigorous, sustained schedule of teaching God's Word for such a prolonged period of time? Because Paul believed that it was imperative for the Word of God to be taught so people would have a foundation on which to build their lives. This was particularly true for the new believers who had been saved out of paganism and had no idea what the Word of God said about right and wrong. They literally needed someone to take them to school to establish them in the principles of good Christian doctrine.

That's what sound Bible doctrine does — it *establishes a foundation*. And that's why, as we're going to see in the pages of this book, Hebrews 6:1,2 says *we must have the foundational doctrines of Christ established in our lives.*

An Honest Look at the Modern Church

In light of this fact, please allow me to be frank with you from the outset. I am very concerned about the state of the modern Church. What bothers me the most as I travel and visit churches, especially across the Western world, is that I often see an absence of good Bible teaching.

In my travels, I hear a lot of good motivational and inspirational preaching. I encounter a great deal of amazing praise and worship music. In fact, it's possible that the Church has never produced better music.

However, I see a real void in the area of solid, foundational Bible teaching. This troubling trend is evident in the Christian community. More and more, believers are beginning to know less and less of the Bible.

This is a very serious state of affairs within the Church at large. When there is an absence of the teaching of Scripture, it creates an unstable, catastrophic situation for the people of God. They lose their ability to discern what is right and what is wrong or to make decisions, based on godly wisdom, about what they should and shouldn't do in their lives. In the pages that follow, we're going to study a passage in the book of Hebrews where this very situation existed.

On the other hand, the Bible is the immovable plumb line. And where the Bible is the immovable plumb line in people's lives, those people become firmly established on the foundation of God's Word. It is for that reason that I am fully engaged in praying for and working toward a revival of the Bible in the Church at large — and I'd ask you to please join your faith and your prayers with mine to that end!

There is nothing more wonderful than the Word of God. It is a platform we can build our lives on. And when the Word of God is exercised and actively working in us, it thoroughly prepares us for life.

Stuck in 'First Grade'

Scholars are not sure who wrote the book of Hebrews. Perhaps it was the apostle Paul; there are some who believe it was written by Barnabas; others believe it was written by Apollos or even Priscilla; and some even believe it was written by Luke. But what we know for sure is that its real Author was God, and it was designed for you and for me!

Whoever wrote the book of Hebrews, this is what we do know: The writer whom God used to pen this epistle was concerned about his readers. We can see the author's concern stated in Hebrews 5:12:

For when for the time ye ought to be teachers, ye have need that one teach you again which be the first principles of the oracles of God; and are become such as have need of milk, and not of strong meat.

It seems these Hebrew believers were *stuck* spiritually. At a time when they should have already been very advanced, they needed to be taught the ABCs of their Christian faith all over again.

Let me start our discussion on this passage of Scripture by sharing an illustration to bring my point home. Let's say that you're walking down a school hallway and you look into a classroom of first-graders, where you see a room full of children sitting at their little desks, studying along with their teacher. But then you notice that right in the middle of all those first-graders is a 60-year-old man, sitting on a little chair at his tiny desk. There he sits, oversized and squeezed into his space, studying the ABCs and other elementary principles, along with all the other first-graders.

If the man had never had the opportunity for an education, it might seem admirable that he would humble himself to attend a first-grade class and learn. However, what if that man had been sitting at that tiny desk for years and years *and years?* Suppose he had been required to repeat the first grade over and over again because he didn't apply himself, he was too lazy, or he just didn't take the need to study and grow seriously? Suppose it is a result of his lack of commitment to learn that he is still sitting in the same chair at the same desk more than 50 years later. Suppose *that* is the reason all of his former classmates have grown up and gone on to have families and careers, and this man is still stuck where he began.

To behold such a scenario would be very bizarre indeed, especially if that 60-year-old man was mentally sound.

That may sound very strange, but that is actually happening in the Church all the time. People come to Christ, and, in a certain sense, they go to first grade spiritually. They are new Christians, and it's time for them to learn "the ABCs" of the Christian faith — the fundamentals of the Word of God. But often because these believers don't apply themselves, or because they are never correctly taught, they never really embrace and apply those foundational principles to their own lives. Therefore, they never graduate to the next level spiritually, and they remain stuck in "the first grade."

PREREQUISITES FOR SPIRITUAL MATURITY

You see, just because you grow older in age doesn't mean that you're automatically maturing. We have a large senior-adult ministry in our church in Moscow, and I can tell you that there are many senior adults who are very immature.

In the same way, just being older in the Lord doesn't necessarily make you *spiritually* mature. You have to apply yourself to wisdom and become exercised by truth. First, you have to *hear* the truth and *receive* it as truth. Then you have to decide to *act on* the truth as a way of life. In this way, you are *exercised* by the truth — the process by which you mature so you can eventually graduate to the next spiritual level.

So I want to ask you: What level of spiritual maturity do you believe *you* are at right now? Would you say you're still in elementary school, or have you attained college level spiritually? Are you perhaps somewhere in between?

Most importantly, what is your spiritual status in the eyes of God?

This is really a very important question. We all need to look at ourselves honestly to understand where we are and what we need to change in order to grow spiritually. No one who remains stagnant *grows*.

Just being older in the Lord doesn't necessarily make you *spiritually* mature. You have to apply yourself to wisdom and become exercised by truth.

Let's look again at Hebrews 5:12, where the writer of Hebrews wrote of his concern that his readers were not where they were supposed to be spiritually:

For when for the time ye ought to be teachers, ye have need that one teach you again which be the first principles of the oracles of God; and are become such as have need of milk, and not of strong meat.

Notice how this verse begins: "For when for the time ye *ought* to be teachers...." This word "ought" is the Greek word *opheilo*, which describes *an obligation*; *a necessity*; *something that should be achieved or accomplished*; *something that is owed*; or *a moral duty*. It refers to a response to something a person has heard or seen. In this particular case, the word refers to Christians who have heard and seen a great deal of God's truth and are now *morally obligated* to be able to correctly communicate and even teach that truth to others. They've been in class so long that they should know the subject inside and out.

That is why the verse continues to say, "You ought to be *teachers*." The word "teachers" is the plural form of the Greek word *didaskalos*. This word *didaskalos* is a very important term here, describing *a masterful teacher* or *someone who is superior in his field of expertise*. It was the very word used in the First Century to describe *rabbis*. So the writer of Hebrews was basically saying to his readers, *"After all the church meetings you've attended and after everything you have heard with your ears and seen with your eyes, you are actually morally obligated by this time to be masterful at your subject."*

That's what the word "teachers" in this context means. The message being conveyed by the writer of Hebrews is clear: *"You need to be superior in this field of expertise — in foundational biblical truths. In fact, with all you've seen and heard, you ought to be like a spiritual rabbi by now — qualified to teach someone else because of everything you've heard and everything you've seen."*

This is a serious statement the Holy Spirit was making to those Hebrew believers, as well as to us today. Think about your own life. Consider the deluge of sermons, teachings, and lessons you've heard in church, on audio recordings, in Bible studies and classes, on the Internet, through social media, etc. If you're at all interested in spiritual matters, you have probably been inundated with the Word of God coming at you from every direction. And given the volume of spiritual information you've ingested over the years, you might conclude that you ought to be quite far along spiritually.

That was exactly the case with the Hebrew believers whom the writer of Hebrews was particularly addressing in this epistle. However, in their case, they were *not* very far along spiritually at all. In fact, the writer went on to say, "…Ye have *need* that one teach you again which be the first principles of the oracles of God."

That word "need" is the word *chreia*, which describes *a lack, a need*, or *a deficit that needs to be met*. The writer was identifying that these Hebrew believers had a spiritual problem: They were saved, but they didn't know the fundamental truths of Scripture they needed to build their lives upon. They were still at a baby stage spiritually.

So when the writer wrote, "Ye have need," he was saying, *"You have a deficit; you have a lack."* Then he identified their need: "that someone teach you the first *principles* of the oracles of God."

These Hebrew believers had a spiritual problem: They were saved, but they didn't know the fundamental truths of Scripture they needed to build their lives upon. They were still at a baby stage spiritually.

The word "principles" is the Greek word *stoicheion*. This word describes *basic elements, fundamentals, or rudimentary knowledge*. The word "first," the Greek word *arches*, describes *the first, the beginning,* or *something elementary*. Early philosophers used this word *stoicheion* to describe the *arche (first)* elements — in other words, the elements without which nothing else could find existence. These are the elements that form the "building blocks" comprising all of constructed creation. Thus, these "principles" are the basic truths upon which rests the entire house of New Testament truth.

In Hebrews 5:12, the word *stoicheion* refers to *foundational* knowledge, or as the verse states it, *"first* principles." So by saying "first principles," the writer was describing *the fundamental knowledge that is required for every believer to obtain before he can advance to a higher level of spiritual education.*

THE SIX 'FIRST PRINCIPLES'

An example in the natural of the "first principles" concept would be a child learning to read. That child can't read deep, intellectually complex literature until he first learns his ABCs and how to read simple English sentence structures in elementary-level literature. Only then can he move on to literature that contains more complex sentence structures and expounds on deeper and more profound concepts.

Let's skip ahead for a moment to Hebrews 6:1 and 2, where we are given what the Bible calls "the principles of the doctrines of Christ" — those first, or elementary, principles that every Christian should know. It says:

> **Therefore leaving the principles of the doctrine of Christ, let us go on unto perfection; not laying again the foundation of repentance from dead works, and of faith toward God, of the doctrine of baptisms, and of laying on of hands, and of resurrection of the dead, and of eternal judgment.**

In this verse, the Bible gives us the *elementary principles* — or as the Greek word indicates, the *starting points* — that *every* believer should know. In other words, this verse gives us the ABCs, the foundational bedrock, of the Christian life.

There are six of these elementary principles:

1. Repentance from dead works

2. Faith toward God

3. The doctrine of baptisms

4. The laying on of hands

5. Resurrection from the dead

6. The doctrine of eternal judgment

These are the ABCs of the Christian life. And when believers do not know these fundamental doctrines, it causes them to struggle and make catastrophic mistakes in their lives.

Had these Hebrew believers who were being addressed learned these foundational doctrines earlier, they would have been further along in their walk with God. But because they had never learned these six basic doctrines, they were still in the "spiritual beginners" class.

This is also a very real issue in the modern-day Church. Many Christians try to act like they are on a very advanced spiritual level. But too often, they don't even know the ABCs of their Christian faith — and that lack of knowledge causes them to make critical mistakes.

An example that comes to mind is from our early years of ministry when Denise and I were still itinerating in America. There was a young man who worked in our ministry. This young man *loved* the whole concept of ministry, and he wanted to be in the ministry. He had passion. He had desire. *But* this young man had never even been water baptized.

I asked him, "Why are you not water baptized?"

He replied, "Water baptism isn't necessary for salvation. I don't even know why we do that."

Many Christians try to act like
they are on a very advanced spiritual level.
But too often, they don't even know the ABCs
of their Christian faith — and that lack of knowledge
causes them to make critical mistakes.

Water baptism is not a prerequisite for salvation, but it *is* a prerequisite for a life of obedience. This young man had never obeyed Jesus' command to be baptized — yet he was wanting to one day have a ministry of his own that would touch the world. He had huge, lofty dreams for his role in the ministry, *but* he had skipped beginners' class. Consequently, much of his spiritual life was off base and it eventually produced real trouble in his life. No one questioned his desire or his passion. But when a person has passion without knowledge, he makes passionate *mistakes*.

First Things First

You have to build a solid foundation before you can function at an advanced level.

I want to give you a natural example of this truth from my own life. When I was an adolescent, I became physically sick and couldn't go to school for nearly half a year. During that extended period of lost class time, I missed a very important time when they were teaching new concepts in mathematics.

I had struggled with mathematics even before this happened, but having missed this very important slice of time during the seventh grade, I found myself utterly lost in math class when I returned to school. They had all covered material I hadn't covered, and it was if they were all speaking a foreign language I didn't understand!

At the end of that school year, I graduated to the next class. But throughout that next school year, I continued to struggle because I hadn't learned the fundamentals everyone else had learned the year before.

Then I went into the ninth grade and faced the prospect of ninth-grade algebra. I remember being so afraid to go to my algebra class! If I'd been lost in math in the seventh and eighth grades, how in the world was I going to do algebra in the ninth grade? And as it turned out, I *wasn't* able to pass in algebra that year — not because I was stupid, but because I had missed *the first principles*. I had missed the rudimentary knowledge that was essential before I could advance to the next level of education.

This is what happens with many believers. They "skip class" when it comes to their "ABCs" — the fundamental doctrines of their faith — yet they try to advance to become "upperclassmen," claiming a high level of spirituality. But because they're not equipped to advance, these Christians subsequently come to wrong spiritual conclusions. They embrace teachings that sound interesting but don't quite fit with the Word of God, and they're not able to discern what isn't right. And the reason they keep coming to such inaccurate spiritual conclusions is that they missed the fundamentals, the first principles, of the Christian faith that are absolutely *essential* for growth.

I'm amazed sometimes at the foolishness that some Christians embrace and believe. I can often see that these same people are very sincere and passionate about the Lord, but it's quite evident to me that a lot of what they espouse as biblical doctrine is just spiritual silliness. Why do people embrace such nonsense? Because they're not established in fundamental, rudimentary spiritual truth — the basic doctrines of Christ that give us our sure foundation.

That foundation of fundamental spiritual truths provides a platform on which to build everything else in our lives. It informs our Christian experience and affects the way we perceive what is right and what is wrong. It tells us what we are to believe and what we need to reject. It gives us tools and instruments by which to make decisions and helps us come to correct conclusions.

That's why it is so essential that you avail yourself of solid teaching on fundamental Bible doctrines in our walk with God. The truth is, you're headed for trouble if you don't have a truly strong, Bible-based foundation in your life. You could end up making catastrophic spiritual calculations — and that is an outcome you want to avoid at all costs.

That foundation of fundamental spiritual truths provides a platform on which to build everything else in our lives. It tells us what we are to believe and what we need to reject. It gives us tools and instruments by which to make decisions and helps us come to correct conclusions.

It's so tragic when people make wrong spiritual decisions that adversely impact their life course, their relationships, and even their destinies in God. Perhaps you know people who have done that. More than likely, you also recognize that they were very sincere when they made those wrong decisions. But how did they come to such erroneous conclusions? They were deficient in their knowledge of the ABCs of their faith, which are required before anyone can move on to higher levels of spiritual growth.

THE CONSEQUENCES OF REMAINING 'UNSKILLFUL IN THE WORD OF RIGHTEOUSNESS'

Now let's return to Hebrews 5:12 and pick up on this urgent message that the writer of Hebrews was conveying to his readers — and to us! Verse 12 goes on to say, "…Ye have need that one *teach* you again which be the first principles of the oracles of God…."

This word "teach" comes from *didasko*, which is the same root word from which the earlier Greek word translated "teacher" is derived. The word *didasko* describes *the systematic learning of the student through the ever-present instruction of a teacher.* So this was the equivalent of saying, *"You need to go back to the first grade and start all over again. You need a teacher who will sit by you and establish you systematically in truth — the truth that you didn't get when you were younger."*

Then the verse continues, stating that these same believers had "…become such as have need of milk and not of strong meat." The word "milk" is translated from the Greek word *gala*, which is simply the word for *milk* or *the substance that is given to sucklings.* It also carries the meaning of *baby food.*

So these believers had been saved a long time, possibly even for decades. Yet the writer of Hebrews basically told them, *"You're so undeveloped spiritually in the Word of God that you're still on milk; you're still a suckling spiritually, unable to consume meat. You are still on baby food!"*

The phrase "strong meat" is a translation of the Greek words *stereas trophes*. A better translation of these Greek words would be *solid food*. These believers weren't able to consume more advanced, solid food. They were still on the milk of the Word, even though they had been saved for a long time and had heard and seen a lot.

The verse goes on to say in verse 13, "For every one that uses *milk* is unskilful in the word of righteousness: for he is a babe."

This word "milk" in this verse is again from the Greek word *gala*. Everyone who is on spiritual baby food is unskillful in the word of righteousness and is a spiritual babe. The word "unskill-ful" comes from the Greek word *apeiros,* which is a form of the word *peiradzo,* and it means *to test.* But when the letter "a" is added at the beginning of the word, it becomes *apeiros,* which means *something unskilled, something untested, something undeveloped,* or *someone who is inexperienced.* So here the writer of Hebrews was saying to you and me, *"The people who are not really established in foundational truths, who are inexperienced in deeper spiritual truths and matters, and who are undeveloped spiritually — these people will come to illogical spiritual conclusions."*

So this verse is actually saying that everyone who is on the milk, or the baby food, of the Word is *undeveloped, unskilled,* and *inexperienced* in the word of righteousness. And it's important to note that this phrase "the word of righteousness" here is portrayed as a very high level of spirituality.

The Church is actually filled with people who fit this description. They ought to be spiritual adults by now, but they are still spiritual infants because they have not been exercised by the Word of God. Consequently, there is a great number of modern-day Christians who are confused about what is morally right and wrong. They remain silent on issues like homosexuality, gender confusion, adultery, fornication, and so forth, that destroy people's minds, emotions, families, and *lives*. And they do it primarily out of confusion or out of fear of being viewed as judgmental. Without the foundation of the Word of God, they are left "blowing in the wind" on many subjects (*see* Ephesians 4:14).

These spiritual "babes" often don't know what the Bible teaches on basic subjects. Many don't even understand what the Bible says about eternal judgment. They think that just because they're in Christ, they will never be judged.

This helps explain why there are large numbers of present-day believers who, like infants, have put a lot of spiritual poison into their spiritual mouths that isn't safe for consumption. As a result, this mixing of truth with incorrect teachings not only weakens their foundation and minimizes their ability to produce fruit that is eternal, but it can also pull them so far off course that it eventually results in spiritual shipwreck in various areas of their lives.

This is what happens when Christians don't know the Bible — they have no foundation to stand on. These rudimentary principles of the Word are essential in order for them to mature and to be able to walk out God's plan for their lives as spiritual adults. So when they lack this foundational knowledge, this verse states how God sees them: They are spiritual *babes*.

The word "babe" is the Greek word *nepios,* It simply describes *a suckling* or *an infant still nursing at his mother's breast.* That is *not* who you want to be spiritually! The next verse points you in the direction you want to pursue: "But *strong meat* belongeth to them that are of full age…" (Hebrews 5:14).

As mentioned earlier, the phrase "strong meat" comes from the Greek words *stereas trophes,* and it refers to *solid food.* Solid food is consumed by adults — those who are of "*full age*" — and it's what is required for an adult to maintain his health and remain strong. The phrase "full age" is the Greek word *teileon,* which describes *an adult with adult responsibilities.*

This is what happens when Christians don't know
the Bible — they have no foundation to stand on.
These rudimentary principles of the Word are essential
in order for them to mature and to be able to walk out
God's plan for their lives as spiritual adults.

This is what we desire for ourselves and for our children, family members, friends, coworkers — for *everyone* we care about. We don't want anyone to stay "in the first grade" for the rest of their lives — not emotionally, not in their talent, not in their vocation, and certainly not spiritually. We want everyone to come to *full age* — prepared to handle every aspect of life on this earth wisely and maturely as adults.

BENEFITS OF SPIRITUAL ADULTHOOD

In Hebrews 5:14, we find that when you graduate spiritually — when you get off the milk of the Word and begin to consume solid food — that solid food nurtures you so that you can begin to think and behave like a spiritual adult. In fact, the verse goes on to say that strong meat, or *solid food*, "…belongs to them that are of full age, even those who by reason of use have their senses *exercised* to discern both good and evil."

This word "exercised" is translated from the Greek word *gumnadzo*. It's where we get the word for "gymnasium," but the literal meaning of this Greek word pictures *an athlete who exercises naked*. This word was used specifically to describe Greek athletes who were completely committed to their preparation, training, and successful competition. So before they trained or competed, they would strip off all their clothes and remove every possible impediment, because they wanted their limbs to be able to freely move without external garments to hinder their movement or get in their way.

This visual example vividly represents the *serious spiritual commitment* required in our Christian walk. We are to be among those who say, "I am so committed to the successful outcome of the spiritual race before me that I am diligently working on removing every hindrance from my life!"

When the Word of God is working in your heart and mind, you are "exercised" by it so you can come to a place spiritually where you're able to "discern good and evil" (Hebrews 5:14). The word "discern" is the Greek term *diakrisis*, and it means *to perceive, to discern*, or *to judge*. As the Word of God works in you, it elevates you to a higher level in the Lord. You don't have to stop and wonder, *I wonder what God's will is in this situation?* You will have already discerned His will because you know His Word and you have been "exercised" by it. You know how to act spiritually because you have grown into a spiritual adult.

We are to be among those who say, "I am so committed to the successful outcome of the spiritual race before me that I am diligently working on removing every hindrance from my life!"

Here's another important point about this word "exercise." The Greek word *gumnadzo* also pictures the *fiercest* kind of exercise. Thus, the writer is referring to truly strenuous spiritual activity. He wrote that when you're exercised by the Word of God — when you commit yourself to allowing the Word to do its full work in you — that process brings you to a position of maturity in which you're able to discern good and evil. We saw that the word "discern" means *to perceive, to discern,* or *to judge.* It also pictures just *good ol' common sense*!

When the Word of God is working in you and your natural senses and faculties are being exercised by the Bible, you will have the ability to perceive what's right and what's wrong. You won't have to stop and think, *I wonder what the will of God is in this situation?* — because you will probably already know it. And the reason you'll know God's will is that you know His Word, which provides that information. You won't have to think, *I wonder what is morally right in this situation?* The Bible is continually working in you, and you've continually been exercised by the Bible, consuming solid food. As a result, you already know what's right and wrong in that situation.

God's message conveyed in these verses is this: When a person is exercised by Scripture, his mind will become so sharpened that he will have both more spiritual wisdom and more common sense than most people. He or she will be able to quickly perceive what is right or wrong in situations that arise.

People who are indoctrinated in biblical truths are simply out in front of the rest of the crowd when it comes to wisdom and common sense. This is exactly what this verse teaches! They are easily able to look at a given situation, doctrine, or statement and say, "That's crazy!" or, "That's right!" because their inner man and mind are so exercised by God's eternal truths that have inwardly and mentally developed them.

As you diligently continue your own spiritual pursuit, you will advance to ever-higher levels of education in the Lord. Your part is to obey the principles you already know. As you're faithful to do that, God will teach you more from His Word about what it means to act spiritually as an adult, handling wisely the affairs of life.

This is the process God has set up for each of His children to undergo. *This* is His will for *you*.

THINK ABOUT IT

It is an architectural fact that the stability and endurance of a structure is determined by the quality of its foundation. And it is a spiritual truth that sound Bible doctrine establishes a solid foundation upon which to build our lives.

Similarly, where there is an absence of the sound teaching of Scripture, instability is created in the people of God. Their ability to discern and make decisions according to godly wisdom is deficient and impaired.

In what areas in your own life do you recognize a need to fortify your foundation on the Word of God to become stronger, more stable, more consistent, and better equipped for life and the responsibilities you face?

The scenario of a 60-year-old adult stuck in first grade — as a student, not a teacher — depicts the crippling effects of not applying effort to grow spiritually. Growing older is not always equal to growing more mature. A deliberate pursuit and application of truth to acquire wisdom is of utmost importance to a person's spiritual development.

Name the ways in which you intentionally exercise yourself unto spiritual growth. How would you honestly evaluate your spiritual status according to God's standards of maturity? What daily habits have you put into practice to develop your mastery of the Bible truths you have received through the years?

Hebrews 6:1,2 gives us the starting points, or the foundational bedrock, of the Christian life: 1) repentance from dead works; 2) faith toward God; 3) the doctrine of baptisms; 4) the laying on of hands; 5) resurrection from the dead; and 6) the doctrine of eternal judgment.

These are the ABCs of the Christian life. Believers who do not understand these fundamental truths will, at best, struggle in their Christian walk — or, at worst, make catastrophic mistakes. Passion and zeal are no substitute for knowledge and wisdom. People who are undeveloped spiritually will come to illogical spiritual conclusions not consistent with the Word or the character of God.

Rehearse your own journey. Do you recognize areas where you were unskillful in the fundamental truths of the Word and you suffered unpleasant consequences as a result? What measures did you take to allow the Scriptures to sharpen you to develop not only in wisdom, but also in common sense?

2

OUR VITAL FOUNDATION

I mentioned in the last chapter that in the very heart of Ephesus, the great Celsus Library once grandly stood in the city's oldest district. It was one of the largest libraries in the world in the First Century when the apostle Paul was ministering there. The biggest library of all was in Alexandria; the second largest was in Pergamum; and the third largest library in the world at that time was the Celsus Library in Ephesus. People came from all over Asia to learn in this renowned place of higher education.

At that time, the entire city of Ephesus was celebrated as a center of education and learning. In fact, as mentioned earlier, it was called the "light of Asia" for that very reason. It was generally believed that whatever was taught and promoted in Ephesus would eventually travel on all the roads from Ephesus into the very farthest parts of the province. Therefore, the city served as the starting place for education and enlightenment to spread all over Asia.

The natural advantages of Ephesus' strategic positioning were replicated in the spiritual realm as the apostle Paul carried out his assignment to establish the Church in Asia. As we saw, Paul taught morning and afternoon just a few steps away from the Celsus Library in what was called the School of Tyrannus (*see* Acts 19:9,10). For more than two years, the apostle taught the principles of the Word of God to all those who came to hear. Paul knew how vital it was for people to be established on the foundation of God's Word — and that this foundational knowledge would then spread from the main roads leading from Ephesus to the farthest reaches of the ancient province.

I have stood many times on that spot where Paul stood and taught in the heart of Ephesus. Invariably my thoughts have turned in the direction of what compelled Paul to teach the Word *day after day after day* during those years. He knew that each believer's spiritual foundation needed to be built strong and stable. He understood the mandate on *every* believer's life to "study to shew thyself approved unto God, a workman that needeth not to be ashamed, rightly dividing the word of truth" (2 Timothy 2:15). And the apostle knew that as he taught the Word and established a strong foundation in believers who came to learn from him in Ephesus, the truth in that Word would travel the roads of Asia and spread throughout the region to transform lives everywhere by the power of Jesus Christ.

LET'S QUALIFY TO 'GO ON'

Paul's conviction concerning the absolute necessity of establishing a strong foundation of the Word in believers' lives should be our rock-solid conviction as well. We've already seen how important it is that we know the basic foundational doctrines that underpin what we believe. In fact, as we discussed in Chapter One, the writer of Hebrews was concerned that his readers didn't really know what the Bible taught regarding some of the very basic issues of the Christian faith.

Christians who fail to learn the fundamental truths of the Christian faith often face struggles down the road as a result of faulty ways of thinking that in turn result in wrong decisions. Many of the twists and turns in the road they encountered would have been avoidable had they just been "exercised by the truth" of those elementary doctrines and applied themselves at an earlier stage of their walk with God. Those basic spiritual truths would have become part of their internal makeup and their way of life, enabling them to make wise decisions and better overcome the challenges and difficulties that can arise just by living in this fallen world. But because they never took the time to learn the basics, these believers are still sitting in a spiritual "beginners' class" — and, more than likely, they don't even know it.

Let's pick up with Hebrews 6:1,2 where this thought continues, and we'll take the discussion further.

Therefore leaving the principles of the doctrine of Christ, let us go on unto perfection; not laying again the foundation of repentance from dead works, and of faith toward God, of the doctrine of baptisms, and of laying on of hands, and of resurrection of the dead, and of eternal judgment.

These are the *starting points*, the ABCs of the Christian life, and the Holy Spirit tells us what our position should be regarding them: "*leaving* the principles of the doctrine of Christ."

The word "leaving" in this verse is from the Greek word *aphi-emi*, which means *to leave it* or *to let it go*. It does *not* refer to the abandonment of truth, but rather the realization that maturity requires pressing upward to the next level *after* one has established himself on a solid foundation of fundamental principles. The use of this word indicates God's desire for believers to grow and move on to the deeper truths of the faith.

This foundational beginning is not a stopping point — it is truly only the beginning!

This is the reason the writer of Hebrews continued by saying we must "…go on unto perfection…." The words "go on" are derived from the word *phero*, which means *to carry* or *to bear*. However, the tense used in this verse paints the picture of *a force that carries one onward* or *a force that bears one further*. It could literally be translated *let us be carried*, and it conveys the idea that as we grow spiritually, the Holy Spirit picks us up and personally carries us forward in our knowledge and understanding of God.

Where is the Holy Spirit carrying us? Hebrews 6:1 tells us that He is carrying us toward "perfection." The word "perfection" is the Greek word *teleiotas*, which refers to *a child graduating from one class to the next until he finally reaches maturity*. This means that until we meet Jesus face to face in Heaven, there is no end to our spiritual growth.

Until we meet Jesus face to face in Heaven,
there is no end to our spiritual growth.

But remember, you can't go on to the next grade until you *pass* the first grade! You have to understand the basic fundamentals before you can go on to the more profound and deep truths of God. Only when the basics are established in your life will you be able to advance.

Laying the Foundation —
Once and for All

The writer went on to write in Hebrews 6:1, "...*Not laying again* the foundation of repentance from dead works...." The phrase "not laying again" is derived from the Greek word *kataballo*, which is a compound of the words *kata* and *ballo*. The word *kata* means *down*, and *ballo* means *to throw*. When these two words are compounded, the new word means *to lay something down*.

The use of the word *kataballo* in Hebrews 6:1 tells us that the elementary principles of the Christian faith should be laid down in our lives like a strong, immovable foundation as soon as we come to Christ. And once this foundation is firmly set in place, there should never be any need for it to be laid down again.

The writer of Hebrews went on to call these elementary principles just that — the *foundation* of the Christian life. He began by saying, "...The *foundation* of repentance from dead works...." This word "foundation" comes from the Greek word *themelios*. It is an early combination of the Greek word *lithos*, which means *stone*, and the word *tithemi*, which means *to place*.

When these roots are combined, the new compound word denotes *something that is set in stone*; *a foundation that cannot be easily moved or shaken*; or *something so solid that it will endure the test of time*. Taken together, these different nuances of meaning are the reason that the word *themelios* came to be translated as the word "foundation."

A Lesson From Life
on Laying a Strong Foundation

I experienced a vivid and unforgettable lesson in what is required to build a strong foundation when we constructed our church building in Riga, Latvia, in 1997-1998. It was the first church building to be built in the city of Riga for more than 60 years. In fact, it was so revolutionary that they called a convention of all the architects of the nation to meet in Riga in order to discuss what a church should look like — because no one in that generation had seen a church building built!

I sat and listened as the architects discussed, "Should it have a belfry? If it has a belfry, does it have to have bells? Do the bells have to be made of bronze? Can they be made of plastic? Can the bells be computerized? What should be in a church building in our generation?"

Meanwhile, we bought the land to build our church. The land we bought was in a prime location, but we quickly encountered our first major problem — because the entire parcel of land was composed of yard after yard of nothing more than deep layers of peat moss! We couldn't construct a building on peat moss, so I learned what was required before we could lay the foundation. We first had to dig and dig and *dig*, looking for something solid underneath all that peat moss that could serve as the base of our building's foundation.

Finally, at a depth of 12 feet — and sometimes even 15 feet deep — we came to a solid bed of sand. But then came the next hurdle to overcome: The building was going to be the size of a football field, and we were going to have to remove all that peat moss — 12 to 15 feet deep! I watched as the bulldozers came and then, later, the trucks as they began to drive away hundreds of loads of rich, beautiful, black peat moss.

And the money required for that stage of construction! I spent many hours laying before God, crying out for every cent to dig that hole! I believed God for the money to move all that dirt, and finally the dirt was gone — and all I had to show for it was the biggest hole in the nation. We had run out of money.

I'd walk around the hole and the devil would speak to me. He'd even quote Scripture: *"Oh, you're just like the man who began to build a tower but didn't count the cost. You can't finish what you started. The whole nation is going to laugh at you because all you have is a big hole."*

I cried out to God for deliverance, and the snow fell. I was so thankful for the snow because it was an excuse to explain why we stopped building. You can't build when you have a big hole filled with snow! I just loved that snow. And the rest of the winter, I prayed to God for money to show up so we could begin to build the foundation in the spring.

By the time spring came, we had the money, and the next stages began. Hundreds of trucks began to bring in the rock and sand. More rock, more sand — the trucks just kept coming, filling up that enormous hole to make a solid foundation for the building that was to come.

Finally, that stage was complete. Next came the layer of gravel that had to be spread over that huge expanse of rock and sand. Then it was time to purchase all the rebar.

Rebar is the ugliest metal, yet so expensive — and such a vital element to a strong foundation. The construction crew began to lay that rebar all over the top of that gravel that covered layers upon layers of sand and rock.

Finally, the day arrived when the concrete trucks came, and that concrete began to flow out of those trucks. To me it looked like liquid gold because I was the one believing for all the money needed to keep the process moving forward. Every day I lived on that site, watching them smooth that concrete over the entire surface of the foundation.

Then the crew brought in the big grinders and began grinding the surface to make it smooth like silk. And when they were done — *oh, what a foundation it was!* I have to tell you honestly — I knelt down and kissed it. My life was in that slab, and I was so proud of it!

I would stand way over at one corner of the site, and I'd just gaze on the foundation, thinking, *My gosh! Look at how huge this thing is!* Then I'd walk over to another part to see what the foundation looked like from another angle. I was just so proud of that foundation!

The day finally came when the metal arrived — 55 containers shipped from America. That was a huge testimony in itself! We'd had the entire building fabricated in Tennessee and shipped to the other side of the world for a fraction of what it would have cost to purchase metal in Latvia. But while it was en route to us on the other side of the world, somebody high up in the Latvian government stood against us so we could not receive the metal. We had metal on a ship in the middle of the Atlantic, and we didn't have the permission to receive it.

When they were done — *oh, what a foundation it was!*
I have to tell you honestly — I knelt down and kissed it.
My life was in that slab, and I was so proud of it!

But God! One day at home the telephone rang, and it was the U.S. Consul for the United States in Latvia. Denise and I at that time were the longest-residing Americans in Latvia, so from time to time the embassy would call to ask me questions about our early years in the nation. Afterward, the ambassador said, "Mr. Renner, is there anything we can do for you today?"

I said, "Well, since you asked — we do have this little problem with 55 containers on a ship in the middle of the Atlantic that the government is not going to let us receive. Someone high up in government is upset because we're building the biggest Protestant church in the history of this nation." The U.S. Consul said, "I'll make sure you get your containers. We will go visit the Latvian government together."

When the U.S. Consul and I walked in the door of that government office, he sat down and said to the government official, "I understand that you're not going to let Mr. Renner receive his metal. Do you understand you will lose all your funding from the United States if you don't let him receive his metal?"

The man in government said, "Well, of course Mr. Renner can receive his metal. And Mr. Renner, is there anything else that we can do for you today?"

God took a situation that was designed for our evil and totally turned it around — stamping us with approval in front of the nation! And when the 55 containers came on site, we flung open the doors, and I kissed the metal too! I was putting my *life* into that building.

Finally, everything was built. It was a fabulous facility. And the day came when they rolled out the carpet. I liked the carpet — but they were covering my foundation with it! That was when it hit me:

No one is even going to see this concrete. It's going to be entirely covered with something cosmetic. Yet the real thing is underneath!

Then the foyer was constructed — a massive foyer of beautiful granite with a large atrium that rose 75 feet in the air. It was absolutely beautiful.

But as they began to lay granite on top of all that rock, sand, gravel, rebar, and concrete that made up our strong foundation, I just have to tell you the truth — I didn't want anyone to forget what lay hidden underneath. So I had our names — *Rick and Denise Renner* — inscribed on a big piece of granite so that every person who walked through the front door and over that memorialized inscription would never forget who laid the foundation of that building.

The day finally came to dedicate the new building. What a week it was! Joyce Meyer, Kenneth and Gloria Copeland, Bob Yandian, Marilyn Hickey, Robb Thompson, and so many other friends were there, along with family members who came for the big event. The U.S. Consul was even present! It was such an awesome, momentous occasion.

But here was the problem (in my own mind). When everyone walked in that building, they all looked *up* and said, "Wow!" Not one person looked *down* and said, "Wow! What a foundation underneath this place!" In fact, they were all walking across my foundation, and no one said *one thing* about it!

And do you know what I learned through that entire experience? No one notices the foundation unless there's a problem with it! If there's a problem in the foundation, it puts the entire building in jeopardy.

No one notices the foundation unless there's a problem
with it! If there's a problem in the foundation,
it puts the entire building in jeopardy.

A building can be glorious, yet the foundation is the most important part. It holds the greatest part of the weight and is the most expensive part of the building. Nevertheless, it is also the most inconspicuous part. And if you have done a good job at laying the foundation, your work might be forgotten because of the glory of what gets built on top of it.

SET IN STONE

So imagine what a grace you must possess to be a foundation-layer in the Body of Christ! Your work is the most important work, yet it's the part that people will not talk about later as believers' lives continue to grow into the mighty edifices God has intended them to be.

This was the foundational work Paul was engaged in at the School of Tyrannus for two years. That's why he could later write in First Corinthians 3:10 (*NKJV*); "According to the grace of God which was given to me, as a wise master builder I have laid the foundation, and another builds on it. But let each one take heed how he builds on it."

Laying the foundation was Paul's part. It was the equivalent of saying, "I planted. I started. I laid the foundation. That is my grace. Now another is building on top of it."

Paul was not disturbed that somebody was building on top of his foundation. That's normal. People lay a foundation so they can build on top of it. Paul's part was laying the foundation, and when he was finished with the foundation, his part was over. It was time for the next stage of construction in those believers' lives — and to that effect, he gave this warning: "…Let each one take heed *how* he builds…" (v. 10).

Imagine what a grace you must possess
to be a foundation-layer in the Body of Christ!
Your work is the most important work, yet it's the part
that people will not talk about later as believers' lives
continue to grow into the mighty edifices
God has intended them to be.

This word "how" comes from the Greek word *pos*. In this context, it referred to the "how" of the building process — *the kind of methods, the kind of motivation, and the kind of materials used to build on the solid foundation that has been laid.* In other words, Paul was saying, *"Let every man take heed concerning the quality of what he is building on top of the strong foundation that was laid."*

This takes us back to Hebrews 6:1, which informs us on what is needed to lay the right kind of foundation in our Christian lives — the prerequisite for everything that is subsequently built on top. The writer used that Greek word *themelios* — the word for "foundation," which, as a reminder, means *something that is set in stone; a foundation that cannot be easily moved or shaken;* or *something so solid that it will endure the test of time.*

By using that word *themelios*, the writer was making a vital point for us to get if we are serious about our walk with God. He was saying that our understanding of repentance — and, to take it further, our understanding of *all six* of the elementary principles that the writer goes on to list — should be *set in stone.* These truths should be so rock solid in our lives that we are *immovable* and *unshakable* when it comes to the basic and essential doctrines of Christ.

However, as we've seen, this is sadly not the case for many believers in the modern Church. In fact, a majority of regular churchgoing Christians are most likely not able to provide an accurate definition of these six foundational principles of doctrine. This should be very alarming to us all, because it reveals that most believers are in a stunted state of spiritual maturity. Regardless of their age or how many years they've been saved, most of these believers are like that 60-year-old man we talked about in the last chapter — sitting on his little chair at his tiny desk. If they still can't articulate an answer to such a simple question as, "How would you define this elementary doctrine?" — as far as God is concerned, they are still in *spiritual first grade.*

The writer went on in Hebrews 6:1,2 to list the fundamental doctrines that are essential for us as believers to know in order to lead our lives accurately and come to correct spiritual conclusions about life — the challenges we face and the decisions we have to make.

1. Repentance from dead works

2. Faith toward God

3. The doctrine of baptisms

4. The laying on of hands

5. Resurrection from the dead

6. The doctrine of eternal judgment

A majority of regular churchgoing Christians are
most likely not able to provide an accurate definition
of these six foundational principles of doctrine.
This should be very alarming to us all,
because it reveals that most believers are
in a stunted state of spiritual maturity.

The first fundamental doctrine listed as essential for you and me is *repentance*: "Not laying again the foundation of repentance from dead works."

Let me stop here and ask you: Do you really know what repentance is?

You'd be amazed at how many people can't explain what the word "repent" means. But according to this verse, this is the first fundamental doctrine of a person's faith. If someone doesn't know what repentance is, that person may not even be saved — because it's impossible to be saved without the act of repentance. If a person doesn't understand what the Bible says about repentance, he may not even understand his *need* to repent or be saved.

You can see what a vital element repentance is to the foundation of your faith in Christ!

And the same is true with the second foundational doctrine of *faith toward God*. If a person doesn't understand what the Bible says about faith toward God, that person may not even be saved. This is faith that's rooted in Christ *alone* — not in a person's works, not in *anything* man can do. A knowledge of this kind of faith is absolutely essential in building a right foundation in God.

This same type of reasoning can be extended all the way through the doctrine of baptisms, the laying on of hands, the resurrection from the dead, and the doctrine of eternal judgment. It is imperative that we know what the Bible says about all six of these foundational doctrines. And once we're established in them, we can "graduate" to further realms of learning in Christ.

A Moment To Reflect

Are *you* established in these six foundational principles? If you're not able to answer *yes* to that question when it comes to your own understanding of these fundamental doctrines, that is about to change! I believe you will have a much better grasp of all six of these vital truths before you finish this book — vital understanding that you can help impart to your spouse, your children, your family, and your friends. We'll discuss in-depth each of these principles in the chapters that follow.

When our sons were young, Denise and I would gather them around the table and speak to them about the Bible. We would ask them what they believed and what the Bible says about different subjects. We took every opportunity to speak the Word of God to our children because we wanted them to think right.

When you know the Bible, you think right. When you know the Bible, it gives you a sense of what is right and what is wrong. The Bible gives you common sense. Proverbs 9:10 puts it this way: "The fear of the Lord is the beginning of wisdom...." The fear of the Lord is rooted in your obedience to and alignment with the *words* of the Lord. His truth as revealed in His Word — this is where real wisdom, real knowledge, and real common sense come from.

As we saw in Chapter One, when the Word of God plays a prominent role in your life and you live in obedience to its truth, it brings you to a state of spiritual adulthood where you're able to wisely handle the affairs of life. I can assure you that this is what you want for yourself. You want it for your family and for your friends.

We all want to be spiritual adults. We don't want to be spiritual infants for the rest of our lives who still live only on milk.

So let's now begin a study on each of these six elementary principles that God tells us are vital ingredients for the strong foundation we must have in order to build our life in Christ the way God intends. We can't build the strength and height of the calling and purpose He has ordained for our lives on spiritual "peat moss"! We have to do this *God's* way every step of the way!

The fear of the Lord is rooted
in your obedience to and alignment with
the *words* of the Lord. His truth as revealed
in His Word — this is where real wisdom,
real knowledge, and real common sense comes from.

Never forget the Holy Spirit's admonition through the apostle Paul: "…Let each one take heed how he builds…" (1 Corinthians 3:10 *NKJV*). We're working on building our lives in God in such a manner that we can attain the *full* measure of our divine purpose for being on this earth — "the mark for the prize of the high calling of God in Christ Jesus" (Philippians 3:14)!

THINK ABOUT IT

The foundation of a building is the most important, yet least obvious part of a building. However, without that foundation, the building would have no support and therefore no capacity to remain standing. So it is with the spiritual foundation in your life. When you internalize the fundamental truths of the Christian faith as your own personal convictions, you are better equipped to make wise decisions and to overcome life's challenges to the glory of God.

The next six chapters will strengthen your understanding of the foundational doctrines listed in Hebrews 6:1,2: 1) repentance from dead works; 2) faith toward God; 3) baptisms; 4) the laying on of hands; 5) resurrection from the dead; and 6) eternal judgment. But before reading any further, consider how you would define each one based on your current knowledge.

Explain the practical application, *as you see it,* of each one of these doctrines in your daily life.

The basic principles of the doctrines of Christ are vital to laying a strong foundation that is not easily moved. Once our spiritual foundation is laid, however, the apostle Paul tells us to take heed how we build upon it (*see* 1 Corinthians 3:10).

What you give your attention to determines what you believe. Your beliefs determine what information you will act upon to build your life. You must *choose* how you will build — whether on the bedrock of Scripture and sound doctrine or on something else.

What sits at the very core of your beliefs? Is it the solid rock of God's Word, or the sinking sand of a favorite set of beliefs and standards (*see* Matthew 7:24-27)?

How prominent of a place does the Word of God occupy in your life? Take some time to review your spiritual diet and exercise by writing down your current daily Bible-reading and prayer habits.

Are you strong and stable in some areas of your life, yet find yourself inconsistent and struggling in other areas? It's not the truth you know, but the truth you *put into practice* that determines your strength, stability, and capacity not only to endure, but also to advance in life.

3

REPENTANCE — WHAT IT IS, WHAT IT ISN'T, AND HOW TO DO IT

The first elementary principle that the writer of Hebrews listed was "…the foundation of repentance from dead works…" (Hebrews 6:1). As we have seen, this word "foundation" is the Greek word *themelios*. It is an early combination of the Greek word *lithos*, which means *stone*, and the word *tithemi*, which means *to place*. When these roots are combined, the new compound word denotes *something that is set in stone; a foundation that cannot be easily moved or shaken*; or *something so solid that it will endure the test of time*.

Once again, this means that this issue of repentance is so vital and so paramount in our lives that our understanding of it should be *set in stone*. However, over my years in ministry, I've come to realize that many *do* need to be taught again regarding this essential doctrine because they were never properly taught it in the first place.

The truth is, the vast majority of people in the Church are woefully lacking in knowledge of what true repentance is or why it's so foundational and necessary to the Christian walk. Sadly, the concept of repentance is all too often misrepresented and misunderstood in the Church today, even though it is an elementary tenet of our faith.

Many believers equate the act of repentance with remorse. Or they believe that repentance is simply a spiritual "get-out-of-jail-free card" that allows them to admit fault, ask for forgiveness, and then dive right back into the same sin time and time again. However, these assumptions could not be further from the truth, and Christians who believe this way open their lives wide to attacks from the enemy.

So What *Does* the Word 'Repent' Mean?

So let's look further into what it actually means to *repent*. This word is a very important New Testament word. The first instances where it is used in the New Testament are in Matthew 3:2, Mark 1:4, and Luke 3:3, where we are told that John the Baptist preached: "…*Repent* ye: for the kingdom of heaven is at hand" (Matthew 3:2).

The ministry of John the Baptist was literally launched with that one word "repent." According to John's preaching, the only way to enter into the Kingdom of Heaven was through repentance. Jesus also began His public ministry with that very same word when He said in His first sermon, "…*Repent:* for the kingdom of heaven is at hand" (Matthew 4:17). Then in Acts 2:38, we see that Peter launched his preaching ministry on the Day of Pentecost with the same requirement of repentance when he told his audience, "*Repent.*"

Jesus, John the Baptist, and Peter all understood the same truth: The only way you can begin a relationship with God is through the act of repentance. That is the starting point for every person who wishes to enter into a relationship with God. In fact, it is so foundational to beginning one's relationship with God that if a person has never repented, he has never been saved.

Repentance is the "birth canal" through which people enter the Kingdom of God. In other words, it is the only way a person can be truly delivered from the kingdom of darkness and to emerge spiritually reborn and filled with the God-kind of life.

The word "repent" that was used by John the Baptist, Jesus, and Peter is the Greek word *metanoeo*. It is a compound of the words *meta* and *nous*. The word *meta* means *a turn* or *a change*, and the word *nous* refers to *the mind*. When these two words are compounded, the new word describes in its most basic sense *a change of mind* or *a complete conversion*. This word *metanoeo* reflects *a turn, a change of direction, a new course, a completely altered view of life and behavior*, or *a decision to believe, think, and act differently.*

Repentance is the "birth canal" through which
people enter the Kingdom of God. In other words,
it is the only way a person can be truly delivered
from the kingdom of darkness and to emerge spiritually
reborn and filled with the God-kind of life.

In the Old Testament Septuagint and in Classical Greek language, this word *metanoeo* is used by prophets who called on their people *to turn away from evil and turn toward the way of the Lord, changing one's attitudes and ways.* In the New Testament, this word is used often to denote *a complete, radical, total change.*

Repentance is not the mere acceptance of a new philosophy or new idea. It is actually a decision made *to completely change one's thoughts, behavior, and actions* or *to entirely turn around in the way one is thinking, believing, or living.* Thus, the word "repent" in the New Testament gives the image of a person changing from top to bottom. *It is a conversion to truth so deep that it results in a total transformation wholly affecting every part of a person's life.*

Total Life Transformation

This idea of an across-the-board transformation is intrinsic to the word "repent." In fact, if there is no transformation, change of behavior, or change of desire in a person who claims to have repented, it is doubtful that true repentance has occurred, no matter what the person claims.

Although real repentance begins with a decision to make an about-face and to change, its *proof* can be witnessed as a person's outward conduct complies with that decision. This is not someone just *saying* he wants to change — this is someone *deciding* to be different, *deciding* to turn, *deciding* to change. And on the other side of that decision, the person brings forth the fruits of repentance, or a lifestyle change, that proves his repentance is genuine.

That word *nous*, meaning *the mind*, that is contained in the Greek word *metanoeo* is significant. It means that the decision to repent lies in the *mind, not* in the *emotions.* In fact, in this word translated "repent," there is not a hint of emotion. It is a decision of the mind and heart to *think* differently and to *believe* differently that then results in a change of *behavior.*

If there is no transformation, change of behavior,
or change of desire in a person who claims
to have repented, it is doubtful that
true repentance has occurred, no matter
what the person claims.

This is not the same as a fleeting sorrow for past actions; rather, it is a solid, intellectual decision *to make an about-face turn, take a new direction, and revise the pattern of one's life.* Emotions may accompany repentance, but they are not *required* to repent. Thus, true repentance is *a mental choice that originates in the heart to leave a life of sin, flesh, and selfishness and to turn toward God with all of one's heart and mind in order to follow Jesus.*

A prime example of such a *turning* can be seen in Paul's first letter to the Thessalonian believers when he commended them for the way in which they had "…turned to God from idols to serve the living and true God" (1 Thessalonians 1:9). The word "turned" in this verse is the Greek word *epistrepho*, which means *to be completely turned around.*

Note that Paul said the Thessalonian believers turned from idols "to serve the living and true God." The word "serve" is important, for it tells us that the turn they made produced a life change with visible fruit that reflected the change. It's the word *douleuo*, the word for *a servant*, implying that the Thessalonian believers had fully left behind idolatry and had completely dedicated their lives to serving Jesus.

By using this word *douleuo*, Paul informed us that the Thessalonians didn't just *claim* to have repented; they *showed* it by changing the way they *thought* and *lived* and *served*. Their dramatically different outward behavior was *guaranteed proof* that real repentance had occurred.

The Divine Prerequisite — No Exceptions

Many in the modern Church might view this definition of repentance as extreme and try to relegate it to a specific "camp" or portion of the Body of Christ. But just think back to the apostle Paul's fearless statement when he was addressing those Greek intellectuals on Mars Hill: "And the times of this ignorance God winked at; but now commandeth *all* men every where to repent" (Acts 17:30).

Paul's use of the word "repent" in this verse — the Greek word *metanoeo*, denoting *a change of mind* — must have been very interesting to his audience. Paul was appealing to the intellect of these highly educated Greeks. He was reasoning with them to make *a complete and intentional turnaround* from the worship of idols to the lordship of Jesus Christ. Paul boldly told them that this was God's command and made no apology for the truth.

That phrase "all men everywhere" is all-inclusive in the Greek. It embraces *everyone*. It doesn't matter what color or nationality a person is or how high or low his level of education or economic status — God is commanding all people everywhere to acknowledge that they are in sin, make a decision to turn or change, and bring forth the fruit of repentance. There are no exceptions. *God commands ALL to repent.*

God is commanding all people everywhere
to acknowledge that they are in sin, make a decision
to turn or change, and bring forth the fruit of repentance.
There are no exceptions. *God commands ALL to repent.*

If a person never repents of his sin and makes the decision to turn toward God and receive Jesus as his Savior and the Lord of his life, he simply will not go to Heaven. The Bible clearly teaches that repentance is God's requirement for every person on the planet.

Remorse vs. Repentance

Many people think they repent, but they actually don't. An example of this type of common misconception can be found in Matthew 27:3-5, where the Bible talks about Judas Iscariot. It says, "Then Judas, which had betrayed him, when he saw that he was condemned, repented himself.... And he cast down the pieces of silver in the temple, and departed, and went and hanged himself." We know that hanging oneself is *not* the fruit of repentance. So what does the Bible mean when it says in verse 3 that Judas "repented himself"?

That word translated "repented" here is a very different Greek word from the word *metanoeo* that we just looked at. As we saw, that word "repent" means *a change of mind* or *a decision to think differently, believe differently, and act differently.* But when the Bible talks about Judas Iscariot's repenting, it's the Greek word *metamelomai,* which describes *profound sorrow* or *the feeling of being engulfed in grief.* It is a completely emotional word and has nothing to do with the ability to decide or to make a choice. It refers only to being *swallowed up in regret and remorse.*

Judas Iscariot didn't repent. He did not make a decision to turn his life around. He was just swallowed up in sorrow for what he had done, and that sorrow engulfed him until he committed suicide.

I can illustrate this point from my own life. When I was five years old, I got saved — and I knew very well what I was doing, even at that young age. It happened as a result of a series of meetings when an evangelist came to minister at our church. I remember one particular service when this evangelist preached on the subject of hell and was very vivid in the way he preached. With a young boy's vivid imagination, I could just see the flames of hell engulfing lost souls — and that night, I understood that I was a sinner. I became accountable for my life, and I knew that I needed to repent.

Not long afterward, as a five-year-old boy, I finally walked the aisle. I didn't feel any great sorrow for my sin. I was only five years old — what sin was I going to be sorry for? But I knew I needed to make a decision. I knew that I needed to repent and make a decision for Christ.

One reason I knew this so well at my young age was the instruction of my mother, who had faithfully taught me what it meant to repent and to give my life to Jesus and serve Him for the rest of my life. So one Sunday morning when I was five years old, I walked forward to the altar, and I made a decision. I repented. I had a change of mind and came to Christ as my Savior and Lord. From that day forward, I was going to live for the Lord.

It wasn't long after that Sunday morning that I was thrown into confusion about the subject of repentance. I'd watch adults come down to the altar who would weep and wail and nearly empty boxes of tissue as they cried at the altar. I was so moved by their tears. But then I would see those same adults get up and walk out of the church — and they might not come back for a year! Their emotions seemed so real, yet they didn't start coming regularly to church and often there was no visible proof that they wanted to change the way they lived their lives.

I saw this happen over and over and over. And I would think to myself, *Why didn't I cry when I repented? These people are really crying. They feel such emotion, such sorrow for their lives. But I didn't even cry one tear. I just decided to follow Jesus.*

As time went by and I grew up watching certain people come to the altar again and again, I began to understand that some of those people didn't truly repent. They were just sorrowful, filled with remorse for the wrong they had done. They weren't even able to make a true decision to change because they were still so involved in their emotions. (Sometimes a person's emotions can prevent him or her from making a true decision to change.)

These people displayed great emotion, only to get up from the altar and walk out of the church unchanged. As for me, I had simply made a decision. But that one decision made at the age of five years old would set my life course to embark on a journey with God and fulfill His purpose for my life.

So that's what repentance is — *it's a decision.* If it comes with emotion, that's great. But emotion is not a requirement to repent. This is why many evangelistic organizations report how many "decisions" were made during an altar call — because repentance begins with a decision. You don't even have to feel bad about your sin. You simply have to acknowledge, "This is wrong, and I'm not doing it anymore. I'm making a decision to have a change of mind — to think differently, to act differently, and to *be* different from this moment forward."

That's what repentance is — *it's a decision.*
If it comes with emotion, that's great.
But emotion is not a requirement to repent.

And here is the good news: *You can actually decide to be different.* You may not be able to drum up emotions, but you can look at something realistically and say, "I understand that I'm wrong and that God is requiring me to repent." You have the ability to repent at any moment you need to repent. It's in your hands, and it's within your ability to do. And when you make this decision, the Holy Spirit will join as your Partner to help you to carry it out and make the necessary change.

Understanding the Different Kinds of Repentance

Repentance is God's requirement that brings you into the Kingdom of God. That was the initial experience of repentance — when you repented of sin, were born again, and became a child of God. This act of repentance never has to be repeated again.

But repentance doesn't stop at salvation. This is an important truth to remember when reading Hebrews 6:1. The writer of Hebrews was addressing Jewish believers, and, evidently, when many of them sinned, they kept trying to go back and start all over again. In other words, they would repent as if they needed to get saved all over in order to restore their position as children of God.

As believers, we don't have to do that when we miss it and sin after we've been born again. But the very nature of repentance states that we cannot initially come to God, repent of our sin, and then continue to live as we did before we received the Lord.

We sing the old song, "Just as I Am, Without One Plea"[1] — and certainly we do come to God "just as we are" to receive His gracious gift of salvation. However, God doesn't expect us to *remain* the way we are! He expects change, and that is what repentance is all about. With godly repentance, there must be an abandonment of our past and a complete and absolute surrender to the lordship of Jesus Christ, evidenced by our living according to God's righteous standard.

There will be subsequent times in our walk with God when we need to repent and get ourselves realigned with His Word in some area of our lives. But that is *not* repentance for salvation. That is repentance in which we acknowledge that we have gotten off track and we are now deciding to get back on track again.

When the Holy Spirit opens our eyes to those things that are displeasing to Him, we must be willing to repent — to make an intelligent decision to adjust our thinking and behavior to conform to God's ways. It's a conscious choice that we must make again and again throughout our walk with Him in this life: *Will we remain resistant in our attitude and thus defy God's requirement to change? Or will we humbly bow before His holiness and adjust our thinking and behavior to get in agreement with God and His Word?*

---

[1] Charlotte Elliott, "Just As I Am," *The Christian Remembrancer Pocket Book* (Poetry, 1835).

When the Holy Spirit opens our eyes to those things
that are displeasing to Him, we must be willing
to repent — to make an intelligent decision to adjust
our thinking and behavior to conform to God's ways.

I didn't understand this distinction between initial and subsequent repentance when I was growing up in our church. Consequently, I was trying to get saved all over again every time I felt convicted for something I had done wrong! When I felt that conviction, I suddenly didn't know whether or not I was saved. Denise went through the same frustrating cycle when she was growing up in church. We kept trying to get saved again and again and again.

REPENTANCE FROM DEAD WORKS

The writer of Hebrews went on to say in Hebrews 6:1, "…repentance from *dead works*…." Simply put, this phrase "dead works" refers to any works that produce death. It doesn't have to be overt or obvious sinful acts. In fact, it could be religious activity! For example, there are some denominations that teach that a person has to go through all kinds of unscriptural rituals to be saved.

If you trust *anything* for your salvation besides a simple faith in Christ and His redemptive work on the Cross, that is a dead work and it is *not* leading you into life. You will never be accepted in Christ because of religious activity or your own fleshly efforts.

That was part of my problem when I was young. I was trying to do things to prove to God how sincere I was. I kept thinking, *If I can just show God how sincere I am, eventually God will receive me.* But all those efforts were actually dead works that put me in spiritual bondage. Finally, I came to the day when I just rested in the Lord. It's what Hebrews 4:9 calls, "the Sabbath rest for the people of God." I put away my works, and I just rested in Christ.

It is a fact that if you love the Lord, you will do good things that bless others and further the Kingdom of God as long as you live on this earth. But you don't do those things just to curry the favor of God. You simply have the Holy Spirit living within you, and He leads you and causes your heart to desire to do good things that bless others.

If you trust *anything* for your salvation
besides a simple faith in Christ and
His redemptive work on the Cross, that is
a dead work and it is *not* leading you into life.

Dead works can also be sinful acts of the flesh that used to control our lives. The Bible says that we need to *repent* from such dead works.

In Revelation chapters 2 and 3, we see that Jesus told five churches to repent. The people in those congregations were already saved. He wasn't telling them to repent to get saved, because that was something they never needed to do again. He was telling them to repent because, as Christians, they needed to receive the Holy Spirit's correction and make some changes in their lives.

You might as well settle it in yourself. Even though you're a child of God, you're going to be repenting when you get out of line in order to get back on track for the rest of your life.

More times than I can count, I have had to repent because I had a wrong attitude about something. If I didn't deal with that attitude, the Holy Spirit would speak to me and say, *"Rick, how long are you going to tolerate this bad attitude?"* He usually speaks to me very gently, because I made a decision years ago to always be quick to repent. But when the Holy Spirit speaks to me like that, I always understand that I need to make a change.

And that's what repentance is for a Christian.

There are many other "dead works" that we might need to repent of. Just to name a few:

- Overeating
- Speaking in an ugly manner to other people
- Stealing the tithe (This is actually a very serious form of wrong behavior. You need to repent and bring the tithe to your "storehouse" — your local church.)
- Smoking
- Alcohol abuse
- Unforgiveness
- Bitterness
- Gossiping

All of these things require us to make a decision to repent — not so we can be saved again, because we already did that once and for all. But from the point of salvation until we leave this earthly life, we must continually be ready to repent when the Holy Spirit convicts us of areas where we have strayed. This enables us to stay in right relationship with God, with ourselves, and with others.

A Personal Example

I'll use an example from my own life. In 2016, I made the decision that I was going to lose weight. I understood that I was overweight and that if I didn't make a change in my life, I probably wouldn't run a very long race. I had never exercised in my life, but the call of God was upon me and in front of me. God wanted me to run the race to the finish line, but I was literally carrying excess baggage that would eventually stop me from running.

But I didn't come to that decision without some help. God through my family spoke to me, saying, "It's time for you to make a decision to change." I knew that meant God was requiring me to *repent* of eating wrongly and mistreating my physical body.

I didn't cry; I didn't even feel badly. But I knew God was speaking to me. He wasn't requiring me to shed tears or feel badly, as that is rarely profitable. He was requiring me to make a decision to change the way I ate and to intentionally increase my level of physical activity. Since then, I have lost nearly 100 pounds — but it all started with *a decision*. I decided to change. That means I decided to change and to start going a different direction that would lead me to the desired goal — a long, healthy life with the energy to finish my race.

So let's use my example of losing weight to demonstrate what true repentance is. Remember, repentance is a spiritual decision that's made using the intellect. Emotions may be a part of it, but emotions are not required. There's nothing wrong with emotions, but think how terrible it would be if you had to wait for the right emotion before you could change! The word "repent" literally means, *I'm changing the way I think. I'm changing my direction. I'm going to think differently. I'm going to act differently.* It's a new way of thinking that produces new behavior.

I'll never forget that night when Denise and our sons sat down with me and said, "You're not taking charge of your weight, so we're going to help you."

I have to tell you, initially I felt only one emotion, and it was not a positive one! I was angry because I felt like God and my family were trapping me to make me deal with myself. But as I sat in that chair with my family surrounding me, I knew God was trying to help me because I was not helping *myself*. Finally, I yielded and said, "Okay."

The family then told me, "We're taking you to a place where they will help you learn how to eat right and help you start exercising."

I said, "Well, when's this going to begin?"

They said, "We're getting on the plane tomorrow morning at 5:00."

I was totally shocked. My family had an entire plan in place for my repentance!

As we left for the arranged destination, I acted ugly toward Denise the entire flight. I guarantee you that if I'd had to depend on my emotions to make the right decision, I would have never been able to do it. But eventually my heart and mind came into agreement with God and my family that I needed to change — and that's what I did. And that is what repentance is — making the decision to get in agreement with God.

So if you're someone who says, "Well, I just don't *feel* like changing," remember that *feelings* are not required. God is requiring you only to acknowledge what is wrong and then to make a decision to change. You may not initially know *how* to change, but that's the job of the Holy Spirit. If you will just start turning to go a different direction, He will join Himself to you and empower you to follow through on your decision to change.

If you're someone who says,
"Well, I just don't *feel* like changing,"
remember that *feelings* are not required.
God is requiring you only to acknowledge what
is wrong and then to make a decision to change.

As for me during that time of confronting my need to change, I prayed, "All right, Jesus, You are Lord. I am agreeing to change my life."

Again that's really what repentance is — *coming to a place of agreement with God to change.*

Bringing Forth Fruit Worthy of Repentance

In the Old Testament, people didn't have continual access to the power of God like we do. Repentance was simply a decision or a desire. But in the New Testament, repentance always includes outward actions, because believers have the power of God living inside them in the Person of the Holy Spirit.

In Matthew 3:8 (*ASV*), John the Baptist referred to those outward actions that follow repentance when he said, "Bring forth therefore fruit worthy of repentance." We know from this that God is looking for fruit, or *proof,* of repentance.

We see an example of this principle in First Thessalonians, where the apostle Paul was writing about the Thessalonian congregation. They had been a very wicked people, but they had genuinely repented. And Paul wrote of these believers, "For they themselves shew of us what manner of entering in we had unto you, and how ye turned to God from idols to serve the living and true God" (1 Thessalonians 1:9).

Notice that the Thessalonians *turned toward* God. And when they turned toward God, it necessitated that they *turn away from* idols. And they didn't just turn toward God — they turned toward Him to *serve* Him. This was a lifelong commitment. The Thessalonian believers didn't just claim that they had repented, but they *showed* the reality of their decision to change by how they thought, how they lived, and how they served. Therefore, Paul said in essence, *"It was your outward change that was the guaranteed proof that real repentance had taken place."*

You see, repentance is not just accepting what needs to happen. That's just an acknowledgment. Repentance is when you actually make the decision to *turn*. It is a conversion *so deep* that it results in a permanent life change. If there's no transformation — no change of behavior or desire — in a person who claims he repented, it's doubtful that genuine repentance ever took place.

As we've seen, repentance really was a military term that meant *about face*. In other words, it was the decision: "I'm turning around and going in a different direction. I'm making a decision that I'm going to be different from this moment forward."

Repentance begins with that decision to make an about-face change. But the proof that it really happened is in your behavior *after* you make that decision.

> The Thessalonian believers didn't just claim
> that they had repented, but they *showed* the reality
> of their decision to change by how they thought,
> how they lived, and how they served.

Maybe a person had a religious experience, or maybe he learned that he likes the culture of the church and so he changes the way he talks to be more like the people he's around in that church. But if that person never came to a place of repentance that brought a dramatic change in the way he thinks, lives, and behaves, he is on dangerous ground. He's just sitting in church, thinking he's on the road to Heaven. Yet if there has been no inward change, there is no proof that he is saved.

FOUR ELEMENTS OF REPENTANCE

David was under the Old Covenant, but he actually had a New Testament revelation of repentance and forgiveness. His words in Psalm 32:5 (*NKJV*) provide one of the best descriptions in the Bible of how to repent:

> **I acknowledged my sin to You, and my iniquity I have not hidden. I said, "I will confess my transgressions to the Lord," and You forgave the iniquity of my sin. Selah.**

In this verse, David gave us the four parts to repentance:

1. *Acknowledgment of sin.* You cannot repent if you don't recognize something is wrong. So first, David said, "I acknowledged my sin to You. I was wrong. I messed up. I need to change."

2. *Honesty with God.* David said, "My iniquity I have not hidden." When you come to God, don't try to dress up your life. Don't hide the truth. Say, "Lord, I'm just going to tell You the whole situation." God knows the truth, anyway, but when you tell it to Him, you're coming into agreement with Him.

3. *Confession of sin.* David said, "I will confess my transgressions to the Lord."

4. *Forgiveness of sin.* God always responds to true repentance with His forgiveness. "…And You forgave the iniquity of my sin."

We must recognize our sin and our need to change. Instead of trying to hide our sin, we must be honest before God and be willing to change. And we must confess our sin to the Lord. As we follow these three principles of repentance, the Lord takes care of the fourth principle. He releases forgiveness into our lives, which then releases the power of the Holy Spirit on our behalf to enable us to change and bring forth the fruits of repentance.

This is the process that is required for your spiritual growth. The Holy Spirit will be faithful to show you the things that He requires you to change. As He does this, it's your part to acknowledge what He has shown you. Don't hide the truth about it. Confess it to the Lord, and He'll forgive you. Then He will empower you to turn from your wrong words, wrong behavior, or wrong habits so that you can be free.

That is always God's desire for us — that we would be free in every area of our lives. And that's why He tells us in Hebrews 6:1 that our walk with Him starts with the foundation of repentance. After all, if we don't get this first elementary principle right, we don't even have a beginning. But by laying a solid foundation of repentance from the start, we will have the necessary knowledge to stay aligned with God's Word and His will for our lives — all the way to the finish line!

The Holy Spirit will be faithful to show you
the things that He requires you to change.
As He does this, it's your part to acknowledge
what He has shown you. Don't hide the truth about it.
Confess it to the Lord, and He'll forgive you.

PRAYER TO LAY THE FOUNDATION OF REPENTANCE

Father, I thank You in the name of Jesus for the power to change. I thank You that You enable me to recognize those areas in my life that aren't right and that grieve You. Thank You for the precious Holy Spirit, who connects Himself to me, empowering me to turn and to change how I think and how I behave. Lord, I understand that this is not behavior modification; rather, this is repentance — my conscious decision that brings forth life transformation. I yield to the conviction of Your Spirit as He reveals to me what needs to change. In the name of Jesus, amen.

THINK ABOUT IT

Repentance is the "birth canal" through which people enter the Kingdom of God. Repentance is the only way a person can be truly delivered from the kingdom of darkness to emerge spiritually reborn and filled with the God-kind of life.

Do you recall the day you first repented of sin and came to Christ, accepting Jesus Christ as your Savior and Lord? Did your foundational understanding of repentance solidify your faith that you were saved — while at the same time keeping repentance active in your life from a heart desire to live in unbroken fellowship with the Lord? Or do you recognize your need to grow in this area of being ready to repent quickly when the Holy Spirit reveals an area of your life that grieves Him?

The issue of repentance is so paramount that an understanding of it should be set in stone in our lives. Unfortunately, many believers either equate repentance with emotional "remorse," or they view it as a free pass to admit guilt, apologize, and then repeat the same sin over and over. This misrepresentation creates a huge breach in their spiritual foundation and leaves them vulnerable to the enemy's attacks.

The only way you can *begin* a relationship with God is through repentance — turning from your ways to embrace His lordship and saving power. And if you desire to *maintain* unbroken fellowship with Him, it is found the same way — through the turning-around, aligning process of repentance.

Have you ever confused the emotion of remorse for the decision of repentance? Describe the result of remorse versus the result of repentance. Then take time to honestly evaluate the role that repentance holds in your life on a regular basis.

In Revelation chapters 2 and 3, we read that Christ personally addressed the seven churches of Asia. He offered commendations to the churches of Smyrna and Philadelphia for perseverance and faithfulness — but He required the remaining five to repent of their ways or face severe consequences. Jesus clearly identified the attitudes and actions that required repentance: Ephesus performed good works without love for the Lord. Pergamum diluted its doctrine, resulting in great compromise. Thyatira tolerated a cult of immorality. Sardis was full of dead works, with no power of the Holy Spirit. And lukewarm Laodicea received the sternest rebuke of all for its compromise, conceit, and utter lack of concern to pursue Christ's approval or presence.

Think about it: Do you detect any of these qualities within your own life to a lesser or greater degree? If so, tell yourself the truth and acknowledge it before the Lord as sin resulting from compromise and neglect. Then follow through to do what Christ requires of you: *Repent*.

4

'FAITH TOWARD GOD'

I've been to Egypt many times, and when I go there, I enjoy visiting the tombs in the Valley of the Kings. I'm always amazed by one thing I invariably see inscribed on the walls of these tombs — a picture of a set of scales. On one side of the scales is a heart, and on the other side of the scales is a feather. This was the picture of the gods weighing a person's heart and actions in life. The heart represented the person's sins. The feather represented his good works. If his sin was heavier than his works, the person's eternity would be damned.

Of course, the Egyptians as a people or culture were unsaved pagans. But the first time I saw that image inscribed on the walls of the ancient tombs, I thought, *Man has always been afraid of his eternal future and has always tried to figure out how to get ready for it.*

So with that in mind and before we explore the next fundamental doctrine listed in Hebrews 6:1 — that of *faith toward God* — I'd like to begin with a "thought-provoker." I want you to ask yourself: *Suppose I were to die today, and I stood at the door of Heaven. If God asked me, "Why should I let you into Heaven?" — what would I say?*

What do people say when asked why they believe they will go to Heaven when they die? If you ask most people that question, here's how they might answer:

- "I've lived a good life."
- "I've been sincere."
- "I've done nice things for people."
- "I've not hurt anyone."
- "I've given to the poor."
- "I've helped others."
- "I've worked very hard in life."
- "I've educated myself and lived a cultured life."
- "I've been a good parent."
- "I took good care of my elderly parents."
- "I was a church member."
- "I've been water baptized."
- "I took Communion."
- "I gave tithes and offerings."

So many people give these types of answers, and they are all commendable achievements. But *none* of these things saves a person. A lot of sincere, good people who do good deeds go to hell!

It's wonderful that a person does all the things I just listed, but not one of them actually causes him or her to be born again.

If any of the above-listed items is *your* basis for believing that God will allow you to enter Heaven, you need to understand with finality that *none* of them will get you there. Never forget — hell is *filled* with people who did good things and who lived good lives. Doing good deeds does *not* open the door to Heaven!

The Bible says that people who trust in *anything* other than Christ will go to hell after death (*see* John 3:36; John 5:28,29; John 14:6; Acts 4:12; 2 Thessalonians 1:8,9). It's that simple. Never let yourself forget this stark reality. That may not be pleasant to hear, but it is what the Bible says. The only ones who go to Heaven are those who have wholly and completely put their trust in Christ alone.

That is what Hebrews 6:1 means when it talks about "faith toward God": *resting one's faith completely on God, in total trust in God, and not trusting in anything else.*

Never forget — hell is *filled* with people
who did good things and who lived good lives.
Doing good deeds does *not* open the door to Heaven!

You can see why it's so essential to renew your thinking about this fundamental truth if you have assumed in times past that you're going to go to Heaven because you have tried to be good. It's commendable that you have endeavored to be a good person. If you've given to the poor, that's also a good thing to do. You *need* to give to the poor. But that does *not* solve the problem of your eternal destiny. Your problem runs much deeper than that. I pray that by the end of this chapter, you will know beyond a shadow of a doubt the simple truth of what is required of any person to gain Heaven and to shun hell.

A Brief Review —
Foundation First

Let's go further now in exploring the ABCs of faith listed in Hebrews 6:1,2. Remember, we're ensuring that we're established in the basics — the elementary principles of the doctrines of Christ — so we can "leave" them and move on. We want to grasp them and grow in our walk with God and go on to higher and deeper truths — but we have to be able to pass the "basics of faith" test first.

If you don't get these fundamentals right, it's guaranteed that somewhere along the way in the future, you'll make a wrong spiritual calculation that will radically affect your life in a negative way. For example, without "faith toward God," a person is in danger of trusting something other than Jesus Christ as the way to Heaven — and *that* wrong spiritual calculation will have *devastating eternal* consequences!

It is simply essential to thoroughly understand the basics that make up your spiritual foundation. They affect everything else you build in your life with Christ, just as the strength of a building's foundation affects and determines the quality, height, and strength of the building that can be built upon it.

In a major city of the former USSR, there is a very large building that has never been occupied because the builders didn't build the foundation correctly. The planners were in a hurry, and they wanted to build something big and tall. The contractors wanted to prove that they could move more quickly than anyone else and construct a building of this size in a shorter period of time than had ever been done before. And, indeed, they did build a tall structure in record time. However, it is one that can never be occupied because it leans to one side! It still stands in that city as a horrible architectural monstrosity — a huge tower that is lop-sided, off-balance, and off-center. The building is dangerously crooked because the foundation wasn't right.

For decades now, that building has been standing empty in a prime location. *What a waste of time and money and space!* It is used as a massive, ugly "billboard" with gigantic advertisements painted on its tower, and it stands as a glaring reminder of what happens when a building is erected on a faulty foundation.

It is simply essential to thoroughly understand
the basics that make up your spiritual foundation.
They affect everything else you build
in your life with Christ.

The same thing happens in people's lives. They want to go higher in their knowledge of the things of God before they have laid the foundation to build upon. They want to be profound in their depth of knowledge before they have mastered the basics. They haven't laid an adequate foundation for their faith, so the belief system they build on top of the faulty foundation is weak and off kilter. And, ultimately, that belief structure often becomes "uninhabitable," incapable of holding the weight of their divine assignment as they try to fulfill what God has called them to do.

To review further for a moment, we discussed earlier what Hebrews 6:1 means when it says, "Therefore leaving the principles of the doctrines of Christ…." We saw that this word "principles" is the word *arches.* It means *the starting point.*

Every believer needs to come to the place in his spiritual walk where he *leaves* the starting point — the ABCs of the doctrines of Christ — to "go on unto perfection." The word "perfection" is the word *teleiotas,* which describes a *student who graduates from one class to the next class.* This is an ongoing process of education, promotion, and more education. The writer of Hebrews was saying, "Let's go on. Let's not get stuck at this level." However, a believer can't go to the next level of spiritual knowledge and maturity until he grasps the *first* level and passes the first test.

So in these chapters, we are discussing what these fundamental doctrines look like. Understanding and walking in the truth of each of these six doctrines is the prerequisite for passing this "first test" that involves the laying of a firm foundation in our faith. In the last chapter, we discussed the first doctrine listed in Hebrews 6:1 — that of *repentance from dead works.* In this chapter, we will focus on the second doctrine: *faith toward God.*

What Does 'Faith Toward God' Actually Mean?

This particular doctrine may sound like something you've already mastered. You may think, *Oh, I already understand everything about faith.* But what does this phrase "faith toward God" really refer to? It's a foundational truth that is actually very strategic to your faith — and it's not quite as simple as it seems.

First, you have to remember that the book of Hebrews was written to Hebrew believers who had been saved out of Judaism. Being raised in Judaism, they had learned to trust in all kinds of natural things for their salvation. They trusted in the Law. They trusted in circumcision, temple sacrifices, temple taxes, traditions, and their Jewish culture. They trusted in all kinds of religious works to obtain salvation. This was the belief system these Hebrew believers had trusted in for as long as they could remember before they came to Christ.

But our works do not save us. This is why the Holy Spirit presented this doctrine of "faith toward God" as a truth that is absolutely foundational to our life in Christ.

The phrase in Greek is *pisteos epi theon*, which includes the Greek words *pistis* and *epi theon*. The word *pistis* is the Greek word for *faith* and actually describes *faith that is being projected*. This is not a static faith that just sits still or is reliant on itself. This is a faith that is projected somewhere else — and at its point of arrival, the One to whom faith is projected causes it to move *forward*.

This is not a static faith
that just sits still or is reliant on itself.
This is a faith that is projected somewhere else —
and at its point of arrival, the One to whom
faith is projected causes it to move *forward*.

The other Greek word in this phrase, *epi theon*, is a compound word. It includes the word *epi*, which means *upon*, and the word *theos*, which is the Greek word for *God*. When all of these meanings are combined to form the Greek phrase *pisteos epi theon*, it actually means *a faith that is projecting forward and is fully and wholly focused on God and not on anything else*. This faith goes forward for the very reason that God is its *objective*. Thus, this phrase *pisteos epi theon* actually means *a faith projecting toward God alone* — that is, *a faith that leans upon God, wholly trusts in*

God, and does not trust in anything else other than God. It is the picture of complete trust that allows no room for any self-reliance whatsoever.

This is a faith that does not in any form rely on what the Bible calls "dead works" — or, as we saw in Chapter Three, works that *are dead* or works *that do not lead to life.* In particular, we're talking about works that do not lead to *eternal* life.

PAUL'S WARNING AGAINST 'DEAD WORKS'

As the Bible tells us, anything a person trusts in besides Christ is a dead work. And it's important to understand that this issue of dead works is a very serious matter. We see this in Numbers 9:10, where God forbade His people to touch any dead thing. Keep that in mind as we discuss this issue of dead works. Dead works are something we're not even supposed to touch! We're not supposed to go near or have contact with dead works lest we become contaminated by them.

The apostle Paul even wrote about this subject in Colossians 2:21. Speaking of dead works and traditions, Paul wrote, in essence, "Touch not, taste not, handle not — have no trust whatsoever in your good life or in your good deeds." It was the equivalent of saying, "Don't even go near trusting in these things." The Holy Spirit is telling us in this verse, *"Don't touch dead works. Don't trust in them. Don't turn to them. You should have no confidence in any work of the flesh."*

We are not to trust in our works for our salvation. Hebrews 6:1 plainly says we are to have a faith that is *projecting forward.* We have to release our faith, but not based on our actions or our works. We are to release our faith in Christ and Christ alone.

Of course, good works are always healthy and beneficial in a temporal sense, for this life. It's good to help other people, and when we get saved, we will be prompted to do good works.

Dead works are something we're not even supposed to touch! We're not supposed to go near or have contact with dead works lest we become contaminated by them.

Hebrews 6:9 talks about "things that accompany salvation" — and good works are those "things" that accompany salvation. Ephesians 2:10 tells us that we are created in Christ Jesus *unto* good works. But we don't do good works in order to *get* saved. We do good works because we *are* saved. It's a natural byproduct of salvation to want to do good for others, go to church, serve others, and give tithes and offerings.

But good works do *not* merit you any rights to salvation. If you're trusting in your works or your outward actions to be "good enough" to obtain salvation, I need to tell you that you're in trouble. If you don't change your direction, you are headed to hell, because people who trust in their good works to be saved do not go to Heaven. The only way you go to Heaven after this earthly life is over is to trust in Christ and His blood alone.

That's why this phrase "faith toward God" — *pisteos epi theon* — is a foundational doctrine and is so very vital to your faith. In this one phrase, the matter is settled. Our faith is to project forward and lean entirely on God *alone* and on *nothing else*.

I was raised in a denominational church, and later in my early years of ministry, I served in a denominational church. So

I understand how sometimes people who come from a denominational background believe that their actions or their good works have something to do with whether or not they make it to Heaven. They may believe they're okay with God because they have church membership or because they regularly partake of Communion or the Lord's Supper.

> People who trust in their good works to be saved do not go to Heaven. The only way you go to Heaven after this earthly life is over is to trust in Christ and His blood alone.

But this misconception doesn't just run rampant in the denominational world. There are many who attend other kinds of Protestant and even Charismatic churches who trust in a host of things besides Christ and His redemptive sacrifice for their salvation. Like the Jews of the past, they often wrongly believe that tradition or good deeds will somehow save them.

Remember the earlier list of wrong responses to the question, "If you died today, why should God let you into Heaven?" All of those responses rely on the works of man. Yet you'll hear those types of answers from people throughout the Church world. For this reason, many of these churches have church members sitting in the pews who are not born again.

But the fact remains that none of those things will open the door to eternal life with the Lord. The only way you can go to Heaven is to trust in Christ alone, not in any works of your own.

What God may view as "dead works" in your life could actually be *good* works in that it is a good thing that you do those works. But if you're trusting in those good works to save you, you have misplaced your trust. That's why such works are dead — because they cannot lead you to eternal life. Trusting in Christ's sacrificial death and His precious blood is the only guarantee that you will go to Heaven. If you trust in anything but Christ's blood, you are in eternal trouble.

The Bible tells us this truth very clearly in Ephesians 2:8,9: " For by grace are ye saved through faith; and that not of yourselves: it is the gift of God: Not of works, lest any man should boast." We can never boast that we saved ourselves because we were so good in life. The only way we are saved is by trusting in the blood of Jesus *alone*.

LEARNING TO REST IN CHRIST ALONE

So what does it look like when a person makes the decision to trust in Christ *and only in Christ*?

Let me give you an illustration. When I sit in a chair, I don't wonder if that chair is going to hold me. I sit down, placing all my weight on that chair. I am fully and completely resting on the chair, trusting in the chair to hold me up.

This is essentially what it means to place our trust on Christ and Christ alone. We are depending on *Him* to "hold us up." We say, "It's not my works. It's not my activity. I can never do enough to be accepted. So rather than trust in myself and my own efforts, I'm going to surrender to the lordship of Christ. I'm going to put all my faith on *Him*. I'm going to rest with total and complete dependence on Jesus." *That* is the faith that is required for salvation.

When I was a young Christian, I didn't understand this truth, and as a consequence, I really struggled with my salvation and wondered if I was really saved. The reason I wondered is that every week in church, I heard the message that we needed to be saved. I actually was already saved, but I kept hearing, "You need to be saved. You need to be saved. *You need to be saved.*"

Because of what I continually heard Sunday after Sunday, I was continually questioning my salvation. If I asked Jesus to save me once, I know I asked Him ten thousand times. I'd say, "Lord, please save me. Lord, just in case I didn't really mean it the last time I prayed it, this time I'm asking You with all my heart as sincerely as I know how — *please* save me." But a couple of hours would go by, and once again, I'd be doubting my salvation.

Oh, it's such a miserable way to live life! You can't enjoy even one full day of your life, because somewhere during the course of the day, you'll wonder again if you're saved or if you're not saved: *If I die, will I really go to Heaven?*

This was my struggle for many years as I was growing up. It was a form of mental torture.

Then I met Denise, my wife-to-be, and I found out she was raised as I was — continually hearing the question, "Are you really saved?" So Denise also doubted her salvation. There we were, two people who were saved, but struggling to fully believe it. We shared familiar moments of torment when we'd look at each other and ask, "Are we *really* saved?" Each doubt that brought a new round of questions became a recycled phase of our ongoing struggle with the assurance of our salvation that had lasted for years.

This is why people often do good things — because they want their good deeds to be recorded on Heaven's "score sheet." It's amazing all that is done in man's effort to merit some kind of favor with God!

Over those years, I thought if I could just be pious enough or if I could just prove to Him how sincere I was, God would accept me. But you see, all that kind of thinking is a form of works. I was trying to prove something to God in order to "feel like" I was saved. But the truth was, I could never be sincere enough to impress God enough to save me. God saved me because of the blood of Jesus, *not* because of the sincerity of my incessant asking! And I had to come to a place where I finally gave up the struggle and began to really rest on Christ and Christ alone.

I'll never forget the day it happened. In the midst of struggling with that familiar, nagging doubt regarding my salvation, I walked into an empty church auditorium. No one was there. I got on my knees, and I said to the Lord, "This is it. I'm not asking anymore. I've asked and asked and *asked* You to save me. I've probably asked You to save me 10,000 times, and God, I'm so tired of it. If I'm not saved, there's nothing I can do about it." And in that moment, I finally quit struggling, and I rested.

The truth was, I could never be sincere enough
to impress God enough to save me. God saved me
because of the blood of Jesus, not because
of the sincerity of my incessant asking!

That day I gave up my dead works of trying to save myself or to be good enough to be saved, and I simply rested in Christ. And from that day until the present day, I have never had another doubt about my salvation. My faith is *epi theon* — it rests entirely on Christ, not on myself, not on my activities or accomplishments, not even on my sincerity. My faith is on Jesus' power to save me — and on that truth, I rest and I'm at peace.

Laying the Scriptural Foundation

As we study both the Old and the New Testaments, we find out why it is *impossible* for us to save ourselves. Let's discuss why it's so important that we come to this moment of trusting on Christ alone. I'm going to give it to you in eight clear, simple scriptural points.

1. You are born a sinner. Romans 5:12 says that sin entered the bloodstream of the human race through Adam.

    Wherefore, as by one man sin entered into the world, and death by sin; and so death passed upon all men, for that all have sinned.

    Sin is not what you do — it's what you *are*. You sin because you are a sinner.

    A person sins, and has a proclivity to sin, because he or she was born a sinner with a sin nature.

2. According to Psalm 58:3, we immediately "go astray" or begin sinning the moment we're born.

    The wicked are estranged from the womb: they go astray as soon as they be born, speaking lies.

    Sin is not taught to us; it is our nature. And because we are born in sin, we do sin.

I always like to use the example of a fish. When a fish is hatched from its egg, no one has to stop and say, "Oh, we have to give the fish swimming lessons." It immediately swims because fish swim by nature.

The principle applies to our children when they are babies. As cute as they are, it doesn't take long before we see the sin nature reveal itself. A baby might have a fit of screaming over not wanting to go to bed, throw food he or she doesn't want to eat, or learn how to manipulate in ways that work on our emotions. Isn't it interesting that we don't have to teach any of those kinds of behavior to a baby? Why not? Because babies are born in sin, and they eventually come to an age of accountability when they are awakened to their need to be saved.

We don't have to teach a fish how to swim. Fish swim by nature. In the same way, no one has to teach people how to sin. People sin by nature.

Sin is not taught to us; it is our nature.
And because we are born in sin, we do sin.

---

3. According to Romans 3:23, all have sinned. This includes every person, no one excluded.

For all have sinned, and come short of the glory of God.

As a sinner, you can't change yourself. You were born in sin, and sin is in your blood. Through discipline, you may modify your behavior, but changing your behavior does not give you a new nature. You still have a "blood" problem that can only be eradicated by the blood of Jesus.

4. Exodus 34:7 says that every human being is guilty, and God will not clear the guilty.

> **Keeping mercy for thousands, forgiving iniquity and transgression and sin, and that will by no means clear the guilty; visiting the iniquity of the fathers upon the children, and upon the children's children, unto the third and to the fourth generation.**

This is a serious problem for the human race. Sinners cannot enter the presence of God. No one in sin goes to Heaven, and every single person is a sinner. Therefore, God had to solve the problem.

5. Jesus died to pay for the removal of your sin. That's what the Bible tells us in Romans 5:8 — that while we were still sinners, Christ died for us. He paid the price, and His blood was transferred to us.

> **But God commendeth his love toward us, in that, while we were yet sinners, Christ died for us.**

6. Through the blood of Christ, we have received forgiveness. That's what the Bible tells us in Ephesians 1:7.

> **In whom we have redemption through his blood, the forgiveness of sins, according to the riches of his grace.**

Jesus' blood was the price that was paid — the only price that *could* be paid — for our redemption and for our salvation.

7. Jesus sent the Holy Spirit to take up residence within us and give us a new nature. That is why Second Corinthians 5:17 says if any man is in Christ, he is a new creation.

> **Therefore if any man be in Christ, he is a new creature: old things are passed away; behold, all things are become new.**

In the new birth, God has put away the old man. We have been made new by the blood of Christ and have received the Holy Spirit. And when the Holy Spirit comes in, He gives us a brand-new nature; we receive the nature of God. It is a transfusion that changes us, for the new nature He gives us has the power to do away with and override the power of the old nature.

8. Hebrews 6:1 states that only those who trust in Christ alone are saved and will go to Heaven.

> **Therefore leaving the principles of the doctrine of Christ, let us go on unto perfection; not laying again the foundation of repentance from dead works, and of faith toward God.**

This is the faith that is foundational to our Christian life: *epi theon* — faith that rests on Christ alone and not on anything else. People who trust in anything else besides Christ are likely not really saved. I stress again that faith in Christ means one thing only — faith *in Christ*.

Man's Ancient Misconception: 'The Weighing of the Scales'

Just like those ancient Egyptians inscribing the image of a scale on the walls of their tombs, man continues to try to figure out how to ensure a spot in his desired eternal destination, right up to the present time. I remember when Denise and I were first married and we were on staff at a large denominational church. We had people who attended that church actually tell us things like, "I'm going to go to Heaven because I'm a member of the church." Or another variation was this: "I'm going to go to Heaven because I have been coming to this church for 50 years." And then there was this popular one: "I'm going to go to Heaven because I've given offerings."

We heard those types of statements frequently — very often from people who regularly attended church. They basically believed that because they tried to be good, God would overlook what they did wrong. It's that same religious mindset that the ancient Egyptians possessed, only in a different form, and it rationalizes, *"God will weigh the scales."* People who believe this way think that God will calculate whether they did more good or bad in life; then based on how the scales weigh, He will decide whether or not they will get into Heaven.

But a person who thinks like that is going to fail the test. The truth is, there are many people who have attended church most of their lives who have believed similarly and will have a big surprise when they die. They simply won't go to Heaven if they trusted in something other than Christ alone.

I remember years ago when Princess Diana died in a car accident on August 31, 1997, while fleeing paparazzi in Paris. Her sudden death stunned the watching world because she seemed to be an icon of a blossoming young life. Millions of people watched her funeral service, and for a short time, grieving people all over the world were gripped by the abrupt loss of a young woman who one day earlier seemed to have the best this life has to offer laid out before her.

I don't know whether or not Diana had a relationship with Christ. But I remember saying to a friend on the telephone, "Wow, Princess Diana's sudden death really makes me think of how close eternity is to every person. I wonder where she is in eternity right now — *Heaven* or *hell?*" Because her death brought the reality of eternity to my mind, I was simply speaking my thoughts to my friend. His response therefore took me aback as he said, "How dare you ask such a terrible question. How could you be so judgmental? How dare you even ask such a question about such a kind and good person! Of course she went to Heaven. She did so many good things for people."

But my friend misjudged my comment. I was simply suddenly aware of eternity because someone famous had just passed into it, and I felt no judgment. It was just a sobering passing thought because eternity is an immovable reality that every one of us will have to face.

I apologized for asking that question and never discussed eternity with that friend again, because I realized that I had touched a subject that was difficult for him to consider. I have no idea where Princess Diana is in eternity, but my friend's response told me that he thought doing good things for people was enough to qualify a person for eternal life in Heaven. Yet Scripture states that this is *not* enough.

Countless numbers of even good people have died and gone to hell because they didn't die in Christ. It is not about works; it's about the spiritual state people are in when they die. The Scriptures guarantee that if a person dies *in* Christ, he will be *in* Christ for all of eternity. But if a person dies in a lost spiritual state, he or she will spend eternity in hell, apart from God and in an irrecoverable and lost state forever.

We must understand that hell is real and people do go there. In fact, the Bible says that the *majority* of people go there. Jesus made a point of telling us that wide is the way to destruction, and narrow is the way to life — and few there are who find it.

Enter ye in at the strait gate: for wide is the gate, and broad is the way, that leadeth to destruction, and many there be which go in thereat: because strait is the gate, and narrow is the way, which leadeth unto life, and few there be that find it.
Matthew 7:13,14

The way is open for everyone. But in life, the majority of people do not surrender to Christ. They don't rest their faith on Him alone. As a result, they die deceived, saying things like, "Well, at least I was good to my parents" or, "I was good to my neighbors." That's great. *But every person has to have a change of nature.*

Countless numbers of even good people
have died and gone to hell because they
didn't die in Christ. It is not about works; it's
about the spiritual state people are in when they die.

Eighteenth-Century revivalist Jonathan Edwards said, "You contribute nothing to your salvation except the sin that made it necessary."[2] This is what Hebrews 6:1 reveals — that our salvation is because of our faith in Christ alone — faith *projecting toward*

---

[2] Jonathan Edwards quote, goodreads.com, https://www.goodreads.com/author/quotes/75887. Jonathan.Edwards.

Him. There's nothing else we can "contribute" to exact or ensure eternal salvation.

It is absolutely foundational that our salvation is only the result of our faith in Christ. When our faith is in Christ *alone*, we are secure. We are safe. We can rest in our salvation.

Good Works for the Right Reason

Do you see why this understanding of "faith toward God" is so foundational? It doesn't mean you're not supposed to do good works. You *are* — but for a different reason.

Ephesians 1:13 shows us what a miracle our salvation is and how little it had to do with any kind of human effort or work.

In whom ye also trusted, after that ye heard the word of truth, the gospel of your salvation: in whom also after that ye believed, ye were sealed with that holy Spirit of promise.

Notice in this verse that there's no mention of doing any works to get saved. It says in essence, *"You heard the Gospel, and a divine moment came when instantly you repented and believed. And the release of your faith — that's all, just a release of your faith — ignited that moment when the Holy Spirit came in and sealed you."* That supernatural work of the Holy Spirit in the moment of salvation is *absolutely* instantaneous and miraculous.

Ephesians 2:8,9 is a very fundamental passage for us to grasp when laying the foundation of our faith: "For by grace are ye saved through faith; and that not of yourselves: it is the gift of God. Not of works, lest any man should boast." It's not of our own works! Our salvation by grace through faith became a living reality *instantly* — the very moment we believed. That means we didn't work for it. We didn't earn it. We just received it.

Ephesians 2:10 goes on to say, "For we are His *workmanship*, created in Christ Jesus unto good works, which God hath before ordained that we should walk in them." I love the Greek word translated "workmanship." It is the word *poiema*, which is the word for *a masterpiece*. This tells us that when God released His power into us at salvation, we were so completely transformed that we became like His *masterpiece*.

So we're not doing good works to receive God's gift of salvation. We're doing good works because we *did* receive that gift! When we became new creatures in Christ, we received a new nature, the very nature of God, and that new nature gives us the desire to do good works.

So this verse teaches that if we're saved, we will do good works. However, we don't do those good works to obtain salvation. Those good works become the proof that we *are* saved.

What do I mean by "good works"? Here are some examples, but the list could go on and on:

- Being a good parent.
- Being a good spouse.
- Serving others.
- Using your talents to provide a needed service to further the Kingdom.
- Releasing the gifts of the Spirit through your life.
- Witnessing to others.

- Faithfully bringing your tithes into the storehouse (*see* Malachi 3:10) — into the local church God has placed you in.
- Sowing financial seed as offerings toward the work of God's Kingdom as the Holy Spirit leads.
- Finding a place to serve and be a blessing in your local church.

Our salvation by grace through faith became a living reality *instantly* — the very moment we believed. That means we didn't work for it. We didn't earn it. We just received it.

All of these good works are the *fruit* of salvation — they are *not* a way to obtain salvation. If you do any of these things with the hope that they will help you get to Heaven, they become dead works. Even though they are good works in themselves, your wrong motive behind doing these works render them dead. On the other hand, if you're doing these things *because* you have received salvation and your new nature *wants* to do good works to bless others, that's totally different. They are then the blessed fruit of a saved life.

THE HEART OF THE REFORMATION — SAVED THROUGH FAITH ALONE

I'd like to share something relevant with you about Martin Luther, who is accredited with starting the Protestant Reformation. There were actually other Reformation leaders as well, but

Luther is the one who is most well-known. He lived from 1483-1546, during a time when the Church was living in a great deal of darkness.

For centuries in the Roman Catholic Church, the general population had not had access to the Bible. The church leadership had decreed that only the priests could interpret the Scriptures, and as a result, the people lived in spiritual ignorance. Church leaders taught the people that they had to do certain things to merit forgiveness from sin or blessings from Heaven.

The people were required to do so many different things to supposedly merit Heaven. It was truly a horrible state of affairs. They performed endless rituals and religious activity, all the while in fear that if they didn't do more and more and *more*, they would not go to Heaven. And even when people lay dying, they had no assurance that they were going to Heaven because they never knew whether or not they had done enough good works to undo their bad works — to "tip the scales." It was a form of spiritual slavery, and it caused people to live in perpetual spiritual bondage.

The greatest tragedy of all is the fact that the majority of the people who belonged to the Church of that time did *not* go to Heaven, despite the sincerity of their efforts, because they weren't trusting in the redemptive work of Christ. They were trusting in their good works, such as the number of times they climbed stairs on their knees in penitence or the amount of money they paid in church-required indulgences to merit forgiveness. The people's faith was, for the most part, *not* rooted in Christ and Christ alone.

This in no way is intended to imply that there are not many faithful, sincere believers in today's Roman Catholic Church, because there are. And, of course, in the centuries that followed the Reformation, new denominations were established that also included some unsaved people who put their trust in other things besides the redemptive work of Christ to get them to Heaven. But during that time leading up to the Reformation, the situation was dire because of the rampant scriptural ignorance that had been caused by centuries of limited access to the Scriptures for the general populace.

This is why Martin Luther was so revolutionary in his time. As a priest, he saw the great injustice of this religious system and recognized the spiritual slavery it imposed on the people — not to mention the dire eternal ramifications. Luther was disgusted by it all and began studying the Bible with new eyes. He came to understand those six key words in the Bible: "The just shall live by faith" (Romans 1:17). The revelation hit Luther's heart: that we are *not* saved by works; we are saved *through faith and faith alone.* That was a totally revolutionary idea at that time.

Luther wrote down these five principles to reflect the true basis of salvation for every person:

Only the Word

Only Faith

Only Grace

Only Christ

Only Glory to God

The revelation hit Luther's heart: that we are not saved by works; we are saved *through faith and faith alone.* That was a totally revolutionary idea at that time.

That's why the movement birthed out of Luther's actions was called the Protestant Reformation. Those who joined with Luther were protesting the wrong teaching that one could be saved by good works.

When you really understand this foundational doctrine, it makes you *want* to serve God. You're so grateful that He gave you this free gift of salvation that you want to lend your supply to the work of His Kingdom! You want to sing in the choir, be an usher, witness to the lost, and be a blessing wherever you go — but your motivation is different. It's not so you can get salvation. *It's because you are saved and you have a reason to serve!*

So we have seen without any room for doubt that resting in Christ *alone* is absolutely essential to your eternal status. And if you want to enjoy your Christian life, Hebrews 6:1 essentially tells us, *"This is the starting point. You were saved by grace through faith in Christ alone. And as you rest in that, you can really begin to build your life in Him."*

Jesus Christ came to remove our questions and fears about our eternal destiny once and for all. We don't have to try to "weigh the scales" anymore, because the blood of Christ has cleansed us and made us brand-new creations in Him! In that moment of salvation, the Holy Spirit gave us a new nature and we became part of God's family. Our faith is in Jesus and in Him alone.

When you really understand
this foundational doctrine, it makes you
want to serve God. It's not so you can get salvation.
It's because you are saved and you have a reason to serve!

You can see why this is such a foundational doctrine!

PRAYER TO LAY THE FOUNDATION
OF FAITH TOWARD GOD

Father, I thank You so much for Your Word. I thank You that my faith is not in myself or in anything I could ever do to earn Your favor, but my faith is rooted completely in the redemptive sacrifice of Your Son. Thank You that I do not have to work my way into Heaven. Salvation and access to Heaven is Your free gift to me, given by Your grace and received by my faith in Christ and His blood alone. In the name of Jesus I pray, amen.

THINK ABOUT IT

If God were to ask you why He should let you into Heaven, what would you tell Him? Would your litany of reasons begin and end with what you have done?

If your good works are how you justify your worthiness to be given entrance to Heaven, you are mistaken. Your own merits can never address the issue of sin and separation from God. Faith in God alone is the basis for salvation. If you are not established on this elementary doctrine of faith toward God, your trust and confidence will be misplaced — to your own peril. Furthermore, you will not be equipped to move on to other spiritual matters with understanding because this truth is the cornerstone to an anchored life in Christ.

Take the time to write down a personal statement testifying according to Scripture of your own salvation by no other name but the name of Jesus Christ (*see* Acts 4:12). Consider the future of those who trust in their own goodness and not in the redemptive work of Christ — that they are moving toward an eternity without God if they don't come to that same realization of faith in Christ alone. This sobering truth is truly something for you to think about.

Both the Old Testament and the New Testament are clear that it is impossible for man to save himself. If someone were to ask you to explain your faith in God and every man's need for the sin-cleansing power of the blood of Jesus Christ, what would be your scriptural answer? A solid knowledge of this doctrine of "faith toward God" will prevent you from the bondage and torment of condemnation, doubt, and self-effort in attempting to secure the favor of God.

We are saved to produce good works, but our good works cannot produce salvation. By grace we are saved through faith. It is the gift of God, not of works, so that none of us — no matter what we have achieved in life — can boast of what we have done (*see* Ephesians 2:8,9). Good works should be the outflowing of a life of obedience unto God, not an attempt to obtain His attention or approval.

Do you find your confidence in what you do for Christ or in what Christ has done for you? If all you have accomplished in life was stripped away, would you face an identity crisis and not know how to define yourself? Or would you rest in the abiding knowledge of who you are in Him? Be honest as you answer why or why not.

When we cultivate patterns of behavior that stem from fleshly lusts and worldly activities, we readily identify those activities as dead works. But we tend to forget that the Bible says whatever is not of *faith* is sin (*see* Romans 14:23). How easily we can slip into habits of what we perceive as "righteous duty," yet such practices can be based entirely on our own preferences and not *by faith* in obedience to something God has required in our lives.

Human tendency is to "do" something in an attempt to gain God's favor or approval. But instead of deepening our communion with the Lord, these "works" actually promote self-reliance and produce self-righteousness, both of which are thoroughly unacceptable to God.

Pause to consider your ways. Can you identify any area in your life where sinful attitudes and fleshy traits may have been allowed to remain unchecked? Now is the time for you to eliminate them. Also, evaluate your life to find actions or activities that you may feel good about but that God never asked you to get involved in. Do you recognize anything that fits in the category of "dead works"? If so, take time to repent and get these areas of your life realigned with what you know God has asked you to do.

5

THE DOCTRINE
OF BAPTISMS

As we've been discussing, God wants every one of us to grow spiritually and to thoroughly understand the fundamental doctrines necessary for an effective Christian walk. It's really why I wrote this book — and why you're reading these words right now! It's all part of the process of giving ourselves to the learning of Scripture and of key doctrines that are *vital* in fully establishing our lives in Christ on a solid foundation.

So before we study the next fundamental doctrine of Christ, let's again look briefly at what the writer of Hebrews said in Hebrews 6:1: "Therefore leaving the principles of the doctrine of Christ, let us go on unto perfection…."

We all want to go on to higher and deeper dimensions in our walk with God. That's a good and godly desire. But as we've seen, we can't go on until we first have our foundational principles firmly set in place. Otherwise, the structure we build on top of that foundation will be skewed, causing our lives to lean precariously to one side or the other instead of standing straight and tall and strong in the Lord.

I'll give you another example of what happens when a foundation is badly laid — this time from our own front yard at our home near Moscow.

Several years ago, Denise and I decided to renovate the front of our house, and a key part of the plan was to build a brick wall. When completed, the brick wall was beautiful, and I was so impressed with how quickly the contractors built it. However, over a period of time, that wall began to tilt. But there was a good reason why that wall tilted: The builders were more concerned with their speed of construction than they were in ensuring that the foundation was strong enough to bear the weight of the wall. There was no option but to tear it down and reconstruct it from the foundation up because it was so noticeably off-kilter.

As we've seen, this is what often happens in people's spiritual lives. They move too fast before their foundation is firmly set in place. Then as they go on in their Christian lives, they make wrong spiritual calculations that cause their direction to "tilt" and then veer off course.

For example, if you didn't know what the Bible teaches about morality, you could easily make excuses for people's wrong morals. If you thought it was wrong for you to discern the right or wrong of others' actions, you'd always stay on the fence or stay silent when it was time to speak up against unrighteousness or injustice. You'd refrain from ever taking action, and your compromise with the truth could eventually cause you to make moral, ethical, or doctrinal decisions that are wrong. This is the downward slide you can experience if you never establish a firm spiritual foundation.

For me, blatant wrong thinking is not something I struggle with because I've been taught what the Bible says on so many issues. I don't have to stop and wonder, *Well, maybe this or that is okay.* Because the Bible is very clear, I know how I am to respond to most issues that confront society today.

When a believer is well established in biblical truth and that truth is his spiritual foundation, he has a solid platform on which to build his life in Christ. His foundation enables him to know how to think and gives him guidance in his conclusions on many matters. Furthermore, because this believer has a solid foundation, he can move upward in his walk with God and delve into deeper truths, free from concern that his life will go "tilt" along the way.

This is what often happens in people's spiritual lives.
They move too fast before their foundation
is firmly set in place. Then as they go on
in their Christian lives, they make
wrong spiritual calculations that cause
their direction to "tilt" and then veer off course.

That is why Hebrews 6:1 goes on to say, "…Let us go on unto perfection…." That word translated "perfection" is the Greek word *teleiotes*, which as we discussed in Chapter Two, describes *a student who graduated from one level to the next.* This means it is God's intention that no one gets stuck in first or second or sixth grade — or *any* grade, for that matter. He wants every one of

His children to *continually* be moving forward and upward unto perfection. There is always another realm of growth for every child of God!

'One Baptism' vs. 'Doctrine of Baptisms'

Let's move on and look at the next elementary doctrine listed in Hebrews 6:1,2 that the Holy Spirit considered vital for us to know in order to have a strong foundation. It says, "Therefore leaving the principles of the doctrine of Christ, let us go on unto perfection; not laying again the foundation of repentance from dead works, and of faith toward God, *of the doctrine of baptisms....*"

Notice that the phrase "doctrine of baptisms" doesn't say the "doctrine of *baptism*"; it specifically says "the doctrine of *baptisms*" — plural. That's very interesting to note because in Ephesians 4:5, the apostle Paul wrote that there is "one Lord, one faith, *one baptism*." So in one verse, the Bible tells us there is "one baptism," and in another verse, it says there are multiple "baptisms." Is this a conflict? You can rest assured that there is no conflict in Scripture and that there is not a conflict here.

First, we must understand what the apostle Paul referred to in Ephesians 4:5 when he said, "One Lord, one faith, one baptism." The "one baptism" Paul wrote about in this verse is a divine transaction that occurs the very moment a person is miraculously converted. I'll explain more about this initial baptism later. But for now, I want to mention that after this "one baptism," there are two additional baptisms that God has designed for every believer to experience. We're going to cover all three of these baptisms in this chapter, because all are foundational for you to know and experience so you can grow in your walk with God as He intends.

'Dip and Dye'

Before we go further in our discussion of the three different baptisms in a Christian's life, I first want to give you a new insight into the meaning of the word "baptism." This word is a translation of the Greek word *baptidzo*, which means *to wash, to dip,* or *to be fully immersed by someone into something.* But the oldest historical usage of this Greek word *baptidzo* described what a person did when he wanted to change the color of a garment. That person would dip the garment into a vat of dye and then leave it in the dye long enough for that material to become saturated with the new color. And when the person finally extracted the garment from the dye, the garment had become so saturated with the dye that it came out of the vat a brand-new color, looking completely different than it did before being dipped into the dye.

The original meaning of the Greek word *baptidzo* was actually *to dip and dye* — and that's exactly what happens to us spiritually when we came into Christ. In that moment of salvation when we repented and received Jesus as Lord and Savior, we were instantaneously dipped into and saturated with His precious blood (*see* Romans 6:3,4). The blood of Jesus cleansed us and so completely changed us that we became brand-new creations. As a result, we are *nothing* like who we were before (*see* 2 Corinthians 5:17). We were "dipped and dyed" in the blood of Jesus when we came to faith in Christ.

Keep that meaning of the word "baptism" in mind as we proceed to explore what Paul was referring to when he wrote that there is "one Lord, one faith, *one baptism*" (*see* Ephesians 4:5) — which is the only baptism that is essential for one to be saved.

We were "dipped and dyed" in the blood of Jesus
when we came to faith in Christ.

But before we go further, you must understand that for any kind of baptism to occur, three elements are required. First, there must be a *baptizer*. Second, there must be *a person who is being baptized*. Third, there must be *a substance* into which the person is being baptized. All three of these are *essential elements* in any kind of baptism — so important that if someone doesn't understand these three elements, that person will never understand baptism.

THE FIRST BAPTISM: PERFORMED BY THE HOLY SPIRIT

The *first* baptism — the one Paul referred to in Ephesians 4:5 when he wrote "one Lord, one faith, one baptism" — occurred in the life of every Christian the very moment he or she came to faith in Christ. This initial baptism is miraculously performed by the Holy Spirit, who in this case is the One who does the baptizing.

This first supernatural baptism does *not* require your participation. It's something supernatural that takes place the moment you repent and call Jesus the Lord of your life. In that split second, faster than you can blink your eyes and without your even being aware that it's happening, the Holy Spirit Himself *baptizes* or *immerses* you into Christ. You were baptized into the Body of Christ!

The apostle Paul referred to this supernatural act in First Corinthians 12:13:

For by one Spirit are we all baptized into one body, whether we be Jews or Gentiles, whether we be bond or free; and have been all made to drink into one Spirit.

Paul again referred to this first baptism in Galatians 3:27:

For as many of you as have been baptized into Christ have put on Christ.

This first supernatural baptism
does *not* require your participation.
It's something supernatural that takes place
the moment you repent and call
Jesus the Lord of your life.

This baptism by the Holy Spirit into the Body of Christ is what Paul referred to in Ephesians 4:5 when he wrote, "One Lord, one faith, *one baptism.*" It is the baptism that comes simultaneously with salvation and is therefore imperative *for* salvation. There is nothing we do to receive this baptism except to repent and to call Jesus Lord; then the Holy Spirit takes over from there. Supernaturally — in some way we do not even understand — He places us into the Body of Christ. The Holy Spirit *baptizes* us into Christ, and from that moment forward, we are *in Christ.* That is *good news!*

THE SECOND BAPTISM:
PERFORMED BY JESUS

Let's move on to discuss the *second* baptism. This second baptism is the baptism in the Holy Spirit, and all that is required to receive it is spiritual hunger and faith. When it is received, it results in supernatural power. In this case, the Baptizer is Jesus, and the medium, or substance, into which a person is baptized is the Holy Spirit. We see this in what John the Baptist said about Jesus in Matthew 3:11.

> **I indeed baptize you with water unto repentance. But he that cometh after me is mightier than I, whose shoes I am not worthy to bear: he shall baptize you with the Holy Ghost, and with fire.**

Jesus repeated John's words in essence as He was preparing to ascend to Heaven, saying, "For John truly baptized with water, but you shall be baptized with the Holy Spirit not many days from now" (Acts 1:5 *NKJV*). What Jesus prophesied occurred on the Day of Pentecost when the 120 who were assembled in the Upper Room were filled with the Holy Spirit.

It is important to note that Jesus baptizes *believers* in the Holy Spirit — those who have already been baptized by the Holy Spirit into the Body of Christ. In other words, those who have already received the *first* baptism are the ones who are eligible to receive the *second* baptism. They are already in Christ — and then they receive the *second* baptism as, by faith, they ask Jesus to baptize them in the power of the Holy Spirit.

I grew up in a denominational church that taught me a great deal about the Bible, and I'm so very grateful for it. As I mentioned earlier, I was saved when I was five years old. According to the Bible, the moment I repented, the Holy Spirit supernaturally placed me into the Church. This was the first baptism, when the Holy Spirit baptized me into Christ.

This second baptism is the baptism in the Holy Spirit, and all that is required to receive it is spiritual hunger and faith. When it is received, it results in supernatural power.

But many years later at the age of 14, I received the second baptism we're talking about — when Jesus baptized me into the power of the Holy Spirit. I was saved all those years in between my salvation and my baptism in the Spirit. If I had died, I would have gone to Heaven. However, I didn't have God's power in operation in my life. I wanted to be a good Christian, but I didn't understand that there was another baptism I needed that would *empower* me to be all God had called me to be. This second baptism is not a requirement for salvation. However, it is a requirement for *walking in God's power.*

Somebody asked me once, "Do you believe you have to speak in tongues to go to Heaven?" No, the Bible doesn't say that, and I don't believe that. You can live your entire Christian life and never be baptized in the Holy Spirit. You don't have to speak in tongues to be saved — you have to be *in Christ* to be saved. That is what is required to make Heaven your eternal home.

Yet even though the second and third baptisms are not essential for salvation, they are not optional from God's perspective. Certainly, the Early Church never treated them like they were optional. Although not prerequisites for a person to be born again, these other two baptisms were required in the Early Church for other reasons. And nothing has changed in how God views the necessity of these two baptism experiences. They remain as critical as they ever were to the building of a strong spiritual foundation!

Let's focus for now on the baptism in the Holy Spirit. For believers who desire to walk in spiritual power, they must have this second baptism, which is available to every believer. When you study the book of Acts, you will find that the early believers didn't give new converts options. They never said, "Well, it would be good for you to be baptized in the Holy Spirit, but you don't have to have it." These early Christians understood that if the new believers were going to walk in power and have victory over sin, they *had* to receive the baptism in the Holy Spirit.

It's a simple thing to receive this gift. All a believer has to do is ask in faith, and Jesus will be faithful to baptize that child of God into the power of the Holy Spirit. Acts 2 describes the first time believers experienced the baptism in the Holy Spirit. It's important to note that the 120 disciples who were in that upper room had already expressed faith in Christ and were therefore already believers. As followers of Jesus, they had already been water baptized, just as He had been (*see* Matthew 3:14-17). But there was still a baptism these believers hadn't experienced, and Jesus had instructed them to wait in Jerusalem until they received this enduement of power (*see* Luke 24:49).

Then on the Day of Pentecost as those 120 were praying and waiting before the Lord, Jesus baptized everyone present *into* the power of God (*see* Acts 2:1-4). This was the first instance of the second baptism, as Jesus immersed His Church in the Holy Spirit in a supernatural display of His power.

This is what Jesus wants to do for any believer today who has not yet received the infilling of the Holy Spirit. He wants to fully immerse every believer into the Holy Spirit, clothing that believer with power to more effectively serve Him and the purposes of His Kingdom.

When you study the book of Acts,
you will find that the early believers didn't give
new converts options. These early Christians understood that
if the new believers were going to walk in power
and have victory over sin, they *had* to receive
the baptism in the Holy Spirit.

In fact, if you look at the pattern throughout the book of Acts, you will find that when people were saved, they were always led immediately into this second baptism — the infilling of the Holy Spirit.

- In Acts 8:14-17, Philip went down to Samaria and preached Christ to the Samaritans. When the apostles in Jerusalem heard about it, they sent Peter and John there, and when the apostles laid hands on the new believers, they were filled with the Holy Spirit. In other words, in that moment of the apostles' touch, Jesus imparted the second baptism to the people as He baptized them in the power of the Holy Spirit.

- Another example of the second baptism following the first can be found in Acts 9:17. Saul of Tarsus (who was later called the apostle Paul) had just encountered Jesus and called him Lord on the road to Damascus (*see* Acts 9:6). This was the moment Saul was born again — and in that moment, the Holy Spirit baptized him into Christ. Then in verse 17, Ananias prayed for him to be filled with the Holy Spirit. That was the moment Jesus baptized Saul in the Holy Spirit — the second baptism.

- Then we see the example of Cornelius and his household in Acts 10:44,45. After hearing the Gospel, all who were present believed the message of Jesus Christ that Peter was preaching — and suddenly they received the second baptism and were filled with the Spirit of God.

  Remember, the moment a person repents and believes in Jesus, the Holy Spirit places him or her into Christ. So when verse 44 says that the Holy Ghost fell on Cornelius and his entire household, that means they had just received that first baptism at the moment of salvation. That qualified them for baptism number two, which followed immediately thereafter as Jesus baptized them in the Holy Spirit.

- Acts 19:5,6 is another biblical example of the second baptism following the first. As the apostle Paul entered the city of Ephesus, he met a group of men he had never met before. Paul preached Christ to the men and the men believed his words, which means the Holy Spirit had just baptized or immersed them into the Church. But the men still needed the second baptism. So Paul laid hands on them, and the Holy Spirit came upon them as Jesus baptized them in the Holy Spirit. This is the pattern from the beginning to the end of the book of Acts.

This is what Jesus wants to do for any believer today
who has not yet received the infilling of the Holy Spirit.
He wants to fully immerse every believer into the Holy Spirit,
clothing that believer with power to more effectively
serve Him and the purposes of His Kingdom.

The book of Acts really is a pattern book, not just a history book. It's where we find the pattern of what God expects to happen in the Church throughout all time. And when it comes to the first and second baptisms, the pattern in the book of Acts is clear: People get saved and receive the *first baptism* as the Spirit of God places them into Christ. At that point, they qualify for baptism number two, and in every instance in the book of Acts, they are always led quickly into receiving that *second* baptism — the baptism in the Holy Spirit.

> The book of Acts really is a pattern book,
> not just a history book. It's where we find
> the pattern of what God expects to happen
> in the Church throughout all time.

This reveals the divine pattern in the Bible that God wants every believer, including *you*, to experience. He *wants* you to have this second baptism. If you have never asked Jesus to baptize you in the Holy Spirit, He has power available for you today. (*See* pages 237-238, "Prayer To Receive the Baptism in the Holy Spirit.") All you have to do is reach out by faith and say, "Lord, please baptize me in the power of the Holy Spirit." If you'll ask, Jesus will introduce you to an entirely new dimension of walking in the power of God.

THE THIRD BAPTISM:
PERFORMED BY BELIEVERS

Now let's explore the *third baptism* that is mentioned in the Bible. Baptism number three is performed by believers. Again, there must be a baptizer and a medium, or a substance, into which one is baptized. In this case, the baptizer is a believer or spiritual leader, and the medium into which one is baptized is water. Also, as we've seen, the Greek word *baptidzo* depicts a *full* immersion, not just a sprinkling of water. This is water baptism as revealed in the Word of God.

This third baptism can occur any moment after salvation. If you had any form of water baptism before you were saved — before you knowledgeably repented of sin and came to faith in Christ with the full understanding of what you were doing — it really doesn't count. You actually need to be rebaptized once you have repented and received Jesus as your Lord and Savior, because true New Testament water baptism only occurs *after* salvation.

This is a very important principle to grasp, because *water baptism is the symbolic burying of the old man* (*see* Romans 6:4). A person's old nature has to be crucified with Christ through the act of salvation (*see* Galatians 2:20) before the person can be scripturally water baptized — because when a person is baptized in water, he or she *buries* the old man. That believer shows forth his death to sin as well as his being raised to newness of life in the act of water baptism.

This is such a critical subject to understand that Paul dedicated *ten verses* in Romans chapter 6 to the subject of baptism.

...How shall we, that are dead to sin, live any longer therein? Know ye not, that so many of us as were baptized into Jesus Christ were baptized into his death? Therefore we are buried with him by baptism into death: that like as Christ was raised up from the dead by the glory of the Father, even so we also should walk in newness of life.

For if we have been planted together in the likeness of his death, we shall be also in the likeness of his resurrection:

Knowing this, that our old man is crucified with him, that the body of sin might be destroyed, that henceforth we should not serve sin. For he that is dead is freed from sin.

Now if we be dead with Christ, we believe that we shall also live with him: Knowing that Christ being raised from the dead dieth no more; death hath no more dominion over him. For in that he died, he died unto sin once: but in that he liveth, he liveth unto God. Likewise reckon ye also yourselves to be dead indeed unto sin, but alive unto God through Jesus Christ our Lord.

Romans 6:2-11

Jesus also showed us how important water baptism is to the spiritual foundation of new believers when He gave the Church what we call "the Great Commission" in Matthew 28:19,20:

Go ye therefore, and teach all nations, baptizing them in the name of the Father, and of the Son, and of the Holy Ghost: teaching them to observe all things whatsoever I have commanded you: and, lo, I am with you always, even unto the end of the world. Amen.

Christ's command to us is very clear in these verses. There are five things we are to do:

1. Go.

2. Go to all the world.

3. Make disciples.

4. Baptize them in water.

5. Teach them the Word of God.

Water baptism is a vital, integral part of this five-part divine assignment. The act of water baptism does not save, but when a person allows the one doing the baptizing to fully immerse him in water — or we could say, when that person is "buried" under the water — it is his public declaration: "My old life is dead. It is buried! And just like Jesus was raised from the dead, I'm being raised out of this water, declaring that I'm going to walk in my new life in Christ from this moment forward!"

And in that moment in time, through that deliberate act of obedience and faith, that believer is marked as a follower of Jesus.

I've noticed over my years of ministry that Christians who skip this step and are never water baptized tend to struggle with obeying God in many areas during the course of their lives. There is a reason for this. Although a person doesn't have to be baptized in water to be saved, he does have to be baptized in water to be *obedient*.

Jesus specifically commanded those who believe in Him to be water baptized. At the birth of the Church, it was the first commandment given to those who, convicted by the Gospel message, asked what they were to do. Peter told the people, "…Repent, and be baptized every one of you in the name of Jesus Christ for the remission of sins, and ye shall receive the gift of the Holy Ghost" (Acts 2:38). In fact, in Peter's statement, we actually find *all three* of the baptisms that are part of every believer's spiritual foundation!

In both of these scriptures — Matthew 28:19 and Acts 2:38 — Jesus and the apostle Peter present the divine pattern on this subject of the third baptism: *Water baptism is to be a believer's first act of obedience.* And the way new believers respond to this scriptural command really determines a lot about their future Christian walk.

Although a person doesn't have
to be baptized in water to be saved,
he does have to be baptized in water to be *obedient*.

Believers who start with water baptism set themselves on a strategic path to be obedient for the rest of their Christian lives. On the other hand, I've seen over the years what happens with Christians who skip or disregard this step in the building of their spiritual foundation — those who say, "Well, I don't really think water baptism is that important." They are the ones who often fall out of fellowship and eventually fall back into sin, or they struggle with being obedient in many areas of their lives. That would make sense, because they argued with the Lord at the very first point of obedience. Their decision — perhaps even innocently — to disregard this foundational step forms a pattern of disobedience in their lives.

This is very important for every believer to understand. For instance, I'm thinking of the man I mentioned in Chapter One, who tried to be deep and profound in his knowledge of the Word and wanted so much to be used in the ministry. But I noticed that he really struggled with obedience in his life. He struggled with tithing; he struggled with different areas of sin.

So one day I asked this man, "When were you water baptized?"

The man responded, "I've never been baptized. It's not essential for salvation, so I've never done it."

"Well," I replied, "That explains your life. You skipped something very important." This man had skipped one of the fundamental principles needed to build a strong spiritual foundation for his life.

Do you see how important it is to gain an understanding of these foundational principles? The man's decision to skip water baptism formed a pattern of skipping other essential matters of obedience in his life.

Make no mistake about it — *it's very important that you obey Jesus.*

In the Early Church, although water baptism was *not* essential for salvation, it *was* considered essential in order for one to walk as a serious disciple. That's why from the beginning to the end of the book of Acts, we find the divine pattern: People were water baptized immediately after they were saved.

- In Acts 8:12, the Samarians believed and were baptized.

  But when they believed Philip preaching the things concerning the Kingdom of God, and the name of Jesus Christ, they were baptized, both men and women.

  Notice how quickly the new converts were baptized. Again, although water baptism was not essential for salvation, it nonetheless was *not* considered to be optional, as it would help frame the new believers' walk of obedience to God. Jesus had commanded it, and the early preachers of the Gospel clearly understood that water baptism was the first step of obedience.

Make no mistake about it —
it's very important that you obey Jesus.

- In Acts 8:13, even Simon the sorcerer was immediately baptized after he believed.

  > **Then Simon himself believed also: and when he was baptized, he continued with Philip, and wondered, beholding the miracles and signs which were done.**

- In Acts 8:36 and 38, when the eunuch heard the Gospel, he repented, believed, and immediately was water baptized.

  > **And as they went on their way, they came unto a certain water: and the eunuch said, "See, here is water; what doth hinder me to be baptized?"… And he commanded the chariot to stand still: and they went down both into the water, both Philip and the eunuch; and he baptized him.**

- In Acts 9:17 and 18, Saul of Tarsus, who had just been saved on the road to Damascus, was immediately water baptized after Ananias prayed for him to receive his sight and be filled with the Spirit.

  > **And Ananias went his way, and entered into the house; and putting his hands on him said, Brother Saul, the Lord, even Jesus, that appeared unto thee in the way as thou camest, hath sent me, that thou mightest receive thy sight, and be filled with the Holy Ghost. And immediately there fell from his eyes as it had been scales: and he received sight forthwith, and arose, and was baptized.**

Remember that Saul had already been saved on the road to Damascus. His eternal state had already been sealed by the Holy Spirit. The Holy Spirit had already baptized Saul into Christ. But Saul had not yet received the second or the third baptism. (*Note:* As you study the book of Acts, you'll notice that sometimes the sequence of the second and third baptisms varies.)

In this case, Ananias laid hands on Saul, and Saul was filled with, or baptized in, the Holy Spirit. Then at the end of verse 18, it says he was water baptized.

So Paul received all three baptisms. Since all three were vital for New Testament believers, we need all three baptisms as well.

- In Acts 10:44-48, the household of Cornelius believed in Christ, and all were immediately baptized.

Notice Peter's question in verses 47 and 48 after Cornelius and his household were born again and filled with the Holy Spirit:

> **Can any man forbid water, that these should not be baptized, which have received the Holy Ghost as well as we? And he commanded them to be baptized in the name of the Lord....**

The apostle asked in essence, "Can any man object to these Gentiles being water baptized, since it's evident they have all believed in Christ?

Once again in this passage of Scripture, we find all three baptisms in demonstration. Cornelius and his household heard the Gospel and believed. We know, based on doctrine, that the moment they believed in Christ, the Holy Spirit baptized them into the Church.

This is the Holy Spirit's invisible, instantaneous work that accompanies salvation. They also were baptized in water and were filled with the Holy Spirit. So all three baptisms happened in two verses. This is the pattern we find again and again in the New Testament.

- In Acts 16:14 and 15, Lydia heard the Gospel from the apostle Paul, and after she and her household believed in Christ, they were immediately baptized.

  And a certain woman named Lydia, a seller of purple, of the city of Thyatira, which worshipped God, heard us: whose heart the Lord opened, that she attended unto the things which were spoken of Paul. And when she was baptized, and her household, she besought us, saying, If ye have judged me to be faithful to the Lord, come into my house, and abide there. And she constrained us.

- In Acts 16:29-34, the Philippian jailer and his household repented and believed in Christ — and afterward, verse 33 tells us they were immediately water baptized:

  And he took them the same hour of the night, and washed their stripes; and was baptized, he and all his, straightway.

- In Acts 19:1-5, when Paul met that group of men in upper Ephesus, he led them to Christ and got them filled with the Holy Spirit. Then verse 5 tells us that immediately, without delay, they were water baptized.

  When they heard this, they were baptized in the name of the Lord Jesus.

Again, you can go to Heaven without water baptism — but the level of victory you have in your life will be affected by whether or not you have been baptized in water. Water baptism is not essential for salvation, but it *is* essential in order to be a true disciple — one who is obedient to the commands of Jesus.

This was the pattern of the New Testament. The early believers understood that this third baptism was a requirement and that it started the pattern of obedience in a person's life. It was also recognized as the moment a new convert joined a local body of believers.

Water baptism is not essential for salvation, but it *is* essential in order to be a true disciple — one who is obedient to the commands of Jesus.

In review, these three baptisms are included in the foundational "doctrine of baptisms":

1. *Baptism by the Holy Spirit into the Body of Christ.* This occurs at the moment of salvation without our participation.

2. *Baptism by Jesus into the power of the Holy Spirit.* This can either happen immediately following the moment of salvation or at any time after salvation.

3. *Baptism by believers into water.* Believers can receive water baptism at any time after they are saved, which in a very real way begins their life of obedience to God.

Remember — it is God's will for you to experience *all three* baptisms and to walk in the fullness of what each one was designed to add to your spiritual foundation.

PRAYER TO LAY THE FOUNDATION
OF THE DOCTRINE OF BAPTISMS

Father, I thank You for my salvation, for that moment when the Holy Spirit miraculously sealed me and placed me — baptized me — into the Church. Thank You for the second baptism, performed by Jesus as He baptized me in the Holy Spirit — an experience that continually gives me the power to walk through every situation of life victoriously. I also thank You for the empowering work of water baptism that helped launch me into a life of obedience.

And, Lord, today I pray for people who have never repented and been brought into Your Body, for believers who have never been water baptized, and for believers who have never been baptized in the mighty power of the Holy Spirit. I know from Your Word that You want every person to receive the blessing of all three of these baptisms, so I release the power of the Holy Spirit to do His work of transformation in people's lives. In Jesus' name, amen.

THINK ABOUT IT

Three essential elements are required for any kind of baptism to occur: There must be a baptizer, there must be one who is baptized, and there must be a substance into which one is baptized. There are also three New Testament baptisms: 1) baptism by the Holy Spirit into Christ; 2) baptism by Jesus Christ in the Holy Spirit; and 3) baptism by believers into water.

Baptism by the Holy Spirit into the Body of Christ is imperative for salvation. Our requirement in this baptism is simply to repent and to call Jesus Lord with sincerity. In that moment, we are "saved" as the Holy Spirit baptizes us into Christ, placing us in the Body of Christ. Do you recall the day you were born again and immersed into Christ? Do you keep the reality of that moment fresh in your heart? As you bring forward the memory of receiving salvation, what thoughts are inspired within you?

On the Day of Pentecost, Jesus immersed His Church in the Holy Spirit, clothing them with power to serve Him and the purposes of His Kingdom. The divine pattern revealed in the book of Acts is that after salvation, people were immediately led into this second baptism — the infilling of the Holy Spirit with the evidence of speaking in tongues. This infilling only takes place after you have been baptized into Christ.

God wants every believer — including *you* — to have this experience that will equip you to be His witness with power. Have you received this second baptism? If you will ask Him, Jesus will immerse you into the Holy Spirit and introduce you to an entirely new dimension of walking in the power of God. Think about it: What are the many ways and the various areas in which you need supernatural enabling in this hour? Jesus Himself has made provision for you to receive it. He knew what you would face and exactly what you would need. If you haven't already done so, why not receive His good and perfect gift of being baptized into the Holy Spirit?

New Testament baptism by water can only occur after salvation. If you had any form of water baptism before you knowingly repented of sin and expressed your faith in Christ, it doesn't count. Baptism in water is actually an outward declaration of the burial of the old man. A person's old nature has to be crucified through the act of salvation before that person can be scripturally water baptized. The spiritual action taking place through the act of water baptism is so powerful, people can emerge from the baptismal waters delivered, healed, and set free from the shackles that clung to them through the old man.

Water baptism does not save. Nonetheless, it is crucial and not optional, as it is among our first steps of obedience to Christ. When Jesus gave the Great Commission in Matthew 28:19 and 20, He issued a divine assignment to the Church. The pattern then revealed throughout the book of Acts establishes this baptism as a subsequent act to salvation. Therefore, immersion in water is a public act of deliberate obedience that declares the one baptized is being "buried" and then "raised" to walk as a follower of Jesus Christ. Adherence to this fundamental principle sets the trajectory for a life aligned with God.

Have you been baptized in water? Did you understand at that time to release your faith to enter into the freedom that newness of life brings? If you did not understand it then, please release your faith now and receive the liberty Jesus Christ died to provide for you.

6

THE DOCTRINE
OF THE LAYING ON
OF HANDS

I'll never forget the evening Denise and I were privileged to share dinner with Oral and Evelyn Roberts, as well as Charles and Frances Hunter. Denise and I were so thrilled as we sat there listening to these spiritual giants talk about raising the dead and the many different miracles they had seen in their ministries. It was an amazing evening that I will always hold dear in my memory.

At some point in the course of the evening, I spoke up and asked, "Brother Roberts, what was the most difficult ministry moment in your life?"

Brother Roberts' answer shocked me! He said, "When I was in Brazil, I ministered at a meeting with a crowd of half a million people. That was one of the most difficult ministry moments of my life."

Most of us would think that would be a *great* moment — to have so many people turn out to hear us minister!

Curious, I asked him, "Why was that a difficult moment?"

Brother Roberts held up his hands and replied, "My ministry works through the laying on of hands — and in that case, I couldn't lay my hands on the people. There were just too many people for me to touch in those meetings."

Oral Roberts understood the power of laying on of hands. That's the foundational doctrine we're going to discuss in this chapter.

'UNTO PERFECTION'

We've discussed at length God's strong desire that none of His children get stuck at any point in their Christian walk. God wants us all to "pass every grade" *the first time* in the school of the Spirit so we can move upward into ever-higher dimensions of our walk with Him. I personally believe that even when we go to Heaven, we'll constantly be moving upward, learning more and more and more. God always wants us to go higher and go deeper, as Hebrews 6:1 says, "unto perfection."

Verses 1 and 2 go on to list those six fundamental doctrines that are the building blocks of our foundation to the Christian faith: "...Not laying again the foundation of repentance from dead works, and of faith toward God, of the doctrine of baptisms, and of laying on of hands, and of resurrection of the dead, and of eternal judgment." As we've seen, if your foundation is not strong, what you build on top of it will eventually lead to some kind of wrong outcome or conclusion that will in turn lead to problems in your life — whether it's a wrong moral decision, an erroneous doctrine, or a misguided spiritual calculation. What you build will begin to "lean"; something will go wrong at some point along the way if your foundation is not right.

I can speak from my own experience that my strong doctrinal foundation has saved me from building my life errantly and off course. There are many choices and actions I didn't even have to pray about because I had the Bible in my life, and this is still true today. The eternal truths in God's Word give me the foundation I need to immediately know what is right and what is wrong on a host of issues.

We all need a firm spiritual foundation. That includes you, your children, your grandchildren, and your friends. If you don't do what is necessary to ensure that the next generations understand these fundamental truths of God's Word, they will grow up without that solid foundation — and somewhere along the way, there will be a bad result.

Something will go wrong at some point
along the way if your foundation is not right.

It bears repeating — every born-again person should be established in these six doctrines. So far, we've looked at:

1. *Repentance from dead works.* You begin your Christian life with repentance, and you'll be repenting the rest of your life. It's essential that you know what the Bible says about repentance.

2. *Faith toward God.* This is faith that is rooted in Christ and Christ alone. This is so foundational that if you don't

understand it, you may not even be saved. It is an absolute cornerstone to your faith.

3. *The doctrine of baptisms.* Again, the word "baptisms" is plural. There is one primary and essential baptism; then there are two other baptisms that are vital to your spiritual growth. As a Christian, you need to understand all three.

Now we're going to move on and study the next foundational doctrine listed in Hebrews 6:1,2 — *the laying on of hands.*

IMPARTATION THROUGH THE HANDS — BOTH GOD AND MAN

It actually amazes me that right in the middle of these six fundamental doctrines is the laying on of hands. Repentance and faith toward God are so crucial to the Christian faith. The three baptisms, resurrection, and eternal judgment — each of these is so *crucial.* And right in the middle of these critically important foundational doctrines, we find the doctrine of the laying on of hands.

Why is the doctrine of the laying on of hands right alongside the other five weighty foundational truths in Hebrews 6:1,2? What is it about the laying on of hands that makes it so vital to our faith?

I will endeavor to answer those questions for you in the pages that follow. But I wouldn't have been able to answer those questions as I was growing up in a denominational environment because throughout my childhood and adolescence, I never once witnessed the laying on of hands. I am not speaking negatively about my church where I grew up, as they taught me so many wonderful truths from God's Word. Much of who I am today in God is due to the teaching I received in that church.

However, our church didn't practice this doctrine of laying on of hands or consider it important. We were taught to believe every word of the Bible, but we sincerely didn't understand the importance of the laying on of hands. In fact, I had never even *heard* about the laying on of hands until years later when I was filled with the Holy Spirit in my mid-teens and introduced to different various Charismatic groups. Those were my first experiences of seeing the laying on of hands demonstrated.

I suggest that you take a moment right now to look at your own hands and meditate on this scriptural reality: *Your hands are spiritual instruments that God wants to use to convey spiritual power and blessing to others.* This truth is so important for you to understand and to firmly plant in your heart and your mind. This is what the Bible teaches, and it was always intended to be a central doctrine of the Church.

Look at your own hands and meditate
on this scriptural reality: Your hands are
spiritual instruments that God wants to use
to convey spiritual power and blessing to others.

From the very beginning of time, God has used the laying on of hands for the supernatural transfer of power, blessing, spiritual gifts, and authority. Of course, hands have no magical qualities in and of themselves. But God in His wisdom designed for hands to be the means of transfer for spiritual goods. The divine transaction takes place when a believer lays hands on another person in faith and the Holy Spirit then imparts whatever is needed to the recipient. This includes healing, deliverance to the sick and the oppressed, and so much more.

It's well established in Scripture that God designed human hands to be His instruments through which these blessings would be transferred to another person. But we can also see throughout the Word that this same principle is true concerning *God's* hands. In the Old Testament, we read often about "the hand of the Lord" coming upon someone. That Old Testament phrase was used to denote a moment when God supernaturally imparted something to a person or a group of people.

For example, the phrase "the hand of the Lord" depicted a moment when God's hand supernaturally came on a person or a group of people to impart power, or superhuman abilities, to perform His purposes. An example is the moment "the hand of the Lord" came on Elijah (*see* 1 Kings 18:46). When that happened, Elijah was so empowered that he was able to outrun the king's chariot. So we see this pattern of transference through "the hand of the Lord" in Scripture even when God Himself is the One being referred to. When His hand comes upon someone, a divine impartation or transference from God to man takes place.

There are several instances in the Old Testament when "the hand of the Lord" performed miracles for or imparted other forms of great blessing to a person or a group of people (*see* Joshua 4:23,24; 2 Kings 3:15; Ezra 7:6,28). On the flip side of that, His hand also sometimes brought judgment to those who opposed His ways or His righteous plan (*see* Deuteronomy 2:15; Judges 2:15; 1 Samuel 5:6).

We still use this terminology today when we say, "I really see God's hand on that person." What do we mean when we make such statements? It normally means we can see a noticeable demonstration of some part of God's nature or power in that person's life because God has laid His hand on him or her and imparted special gifts or abilities. Or we might say, "The hand of God was really on our church service today!" In other words, we're saying that the hand of God was resting on that particular church service in a special way — and where the hand of God is, *something of a divine nature happens.*

THE LAYING ON OF HANDS
IN THE OLD TESTAMENT

The Bible establishes this doctrine of the laying on of hands from the very beginning.

My friend, Keith Trump, an American Bible Society scholar who has been awarded the highest marks for his studies in Hebrew and Greek, shared the following insights regarding the significance of this doctrine that extends all the way back to the Garden of Eden. Keith explained, "Throughout the Old Testament, people both gave and received massive blessings or curses via their hands. On this matter, Genesis serves as the seed-plot containing the whole, all the rest being merely the development of the many grand details infused within it.

"Adam and Eve took the fruit of both the Tree of Life and the Tree of the Knowledge of Good and Evil with their hands. Thus, the Last Adam had his hands nailed to a tree. The hands of Cain wrung the blood of Abel from his body into the ground. Conversely, the blood flowed from the hands of Jesus onto the same earth and now speaks more favorably than the revenge-crying blood of Abel."

We see the first specific mention of this doctrine in Genesis chapter 27 when the elderly Isaac wanted to pass his blessing on to Jacob. Isaac had been blessed by God throughout his life; now it was time for him to give the blessing to his son Jacob. Genesis 27:21-29 tells us how Isaac fulfilled that spiritual responsibility: He laid his hands upon Jacob, fully assured that the blessing would literally pass through his hands into his son. In other words, Isaac understood that *his hands* were the vehicle through which the blessing would pass from his life into the life of his son Jacob — an inheritance of favor and increase that Jacob would walk in from that day forward.

Years later as Jacob (whom God had given the new name Israel) was nearing death, he desired to transfer to his family the blessing he had received from his father Isaac. In Genesis chapter 48, Israel asked his son Joseph to bring his grandsons Manasseh and Ephraim to his bedside. When Joseph did what his father asked, the Bible tells us that Israel didn't just speak words of blessing over his grandsons. He understood that for the blessing on his life to be transferred into their lives, he had to lay his hands on them, because the blessing would be passed through his hands. And that is what happened. In Genesis 48:13-20, Israel laid his hands on Manasseh and Ephraim and the blessing was literally imparted through *his hands* into their lives.

Then as we go to Exodus chapters 28 and 29, we find the ordination of Aaron and his sons to the office of the priest. The priestly garments were placed upon Aaron and his sons. And as Moses anointed them with oil and laid hands on them, the call of God was not only acknowledged — it was also *awakened* in them. In an *instant*, the power of God was activated in their lives and the divine enablement to fulfill their priestly office literally passed into them through the hands of Moses, the God-appointed leader.

Moses understood that *his hands* were the conduit through which the anointing would come on Aaron and his sons.

We also find this principle demonstrated in the ministry of Moses to Joshua when Moses imparted spiritual authority to Joshua by laying his hands on him. Moses could have just said, "Joshua, I'm giving you authority." But that wouldn't have accomplished the deed. Moses fully understood that the spiritual impartation of wisdom and power to lead that God desired to give Joshua had to be passed through Moses' hands. Hence, *the leader's hands* were the instruments through which these blessings passed from him into the younger man appointed to take his place.

The Bible tells us in Numbers 27:18 (*NKJV*), "And the Lord said to Moses: 'Take Joshua the son of Nun with you, a man in whom is the Spirit, and lay your hand on him.'" So God Himself said in essence, *"Moses, you will have to get your hands on Joshua if the anointing is going to be passed to him. It will happen the moment you lay your hands on him. Your hands are the channel through which this transfer will take place."*

Isaac understood that his hands were the vehicle
through which the blessing would pass
from his life into the life of his son Jacob —
an inheritance of favor and increase that Jacob
would walk in from that day forward.

Then in Deuteronomy 34:9, the Bible affirms: "…Joshua the son of Nun was full of the spirit of wisdom; for Moses had laid *his hands* upon him.…" A transference and an impartation took place when Moses' hands were laid on Joshua.

And the laying on of hands continued to hold a significant role for God's people under the Law through those appointed as priests. Keith Trump made these observations:

"More than 2,000 years after Cain and Abel, the Lord masterfully wove the inescapable truth about His power flowing through hands into the fabric of the priestly system. Throughout Scripture, the number 60 points to the reality of God's eternal covenant both embracing and surrounding those receiving it. Thus, the priestly blessing consists of exactly 60 letters. Furthermore, the priests had to employ both hands to impart this blessing. They used two hands because each hand contains 30 bones for a total of 60. Their hands served as conduits through which God manifested the power of His eternal covenant."

It is the way God designed it: *Man's hands are vital to the impartation of spiritual goods.*

The Laying On of Hands in Jesus' Ministry

Luke 4:40 (*NKJV*) is one scripture that reveals the vital role that laying on of hands held in Jesus' ministry:

When the sun was setting, all those who had any that were sick with various diseases brought them to him; and he laid his hands on every one of them and healed them.

This was a big event, because everyone got involved! The entire town literally vacated their homes and converged on the place where Jesus was, bringing all who were sick, diseased, or oppressed to Jesus. It was a large crowd! Yet the Bible says He laid hands on *every single one* who needed His healing touch.

At times in Jesus' earthly ministry, He healed people through different means, such as the spoken word (*see* Matthew 8:5-13; 15:21-28). But Jesus understood that healing and deliverance were primarily wrought through the laying on of hands. He knew that His hands were the primary instruments, or conduits, through which God would impart power, gifts, authority, and physical healing to people.

In Luke 4:40, we see that Jesus wanted to lay His hands on the people who were sick or diseased — because through His hands, a transfer of power would take place that would heal their bodies. It probably took many hours for Jesus to lay his hands on everyone in the crowd who needed healing, but He was willing to do whatever was necessary to be able to lay His hands on the sick and infirm so they could receive the power of God that would make them whole.

Then in Mark 6:5, we learn that when Jesus went to His own village, "...he could there do no mighty work, save that he laid his hands upon a few sick folk, and healed them." Once again, we find Jesus employing His hands to impart healing power.

This is actually a very powerful verse that most people don't comprehend because it isn't well translated. When Jesus traveled to His own town, He came with healing power. He was ready to do there what He had been doing everywhere else — heal all who came to Him who were sick, oppressed, and diseased. But the people in Jesus' hometown were full of doubt and unbelief. They couldn't receive His ministry because they had known Jesus all His life, and their familiarity with Him and His family made it difficult for them to see who He really was. They couldn't get past their own familiar view of Jesus to see from a spiritual perspective who He actually was so they could receive from Him.

Notice this verse says, "And he could there do no mighty work, save that he laid his hands upon a few *sick* folk, and healed them." That phrase "sick folk" sounds like something very minor. But the word translated "sick" is the Greek word *arroustos*, which is the very word used to describe people who were *extremely ill*, perhaps even *comatose*. In other words, Jesus couldn't find conscious people whom He could work with in Nazareth, so He went and found unconscious people! He likely thought, *They're unconscious, so they can't doubt. It's easier to work with the unconscious in this town than with the conscious!"*

And how did Jesus heal these *arroustos* folk? *He laid His hands on them to impart healing power!*

This happened again and again and again in Jesus' ministry. He wanted to get His hands on people. Jesus understood the way God had designed the power to flow. He knew it came through His hands.

The people in Jesus' hometown were full of doubt and unbelief. They couldn't get past their own familiar view of Jesus to see from a spiritual perspective who He actually was so they could receive from Him.

The following are just some examples from the gospels of Matthew and Mark that illustrate how this principle was powerfully demonstrated throughout Jesus' earthly ministry:

- In Matthew 8:3, Jesus laid *His hands* on a man and healed him.

- In Matthew 8:15, Jesus laid *His hands* on Peter's mother-in-law and healed her.

- In Matthew 9:29, Jesus laid *His hands* again on blind people and healed them.

- In Matthew 17:7, Jesus laid *His hands* on the apostles and divinely imparted encouragement to them.

- In Matthew 20:34, Jesus again laid *His hands* on blind people — and as healing power passed through *His hands* into them, they were healed.

- In Mark 1:41, as Jesus laid *His hands* on a leper, power passed through *His hands*, and the leper was cleansed.

- In Mark 8:22, Jesus again laid *His hands* on a blind man. Healing power passed through *His hands*, and the blind man was healed.

As stated in this list, these instances listed of Jesus laying His hands on people are those found just in the books of Matthew and Mark! We could still go through Luke and John and find many more examples. The gospels are simply *filled* with these accounts.

THE LAYING ON OF HANDS
IN THE BOOK OF ACTS

Going on to the book of Acts, we find that the doctrine of the laying on of hands continued to be acted on in the infant Church. This was something the early believers understood. They knew that whenever there was the laying on of hands, some kind of transmission took place. These early believers had grown up learning about this principle from the Old Testament, and they continued this pattern as they walked out those first, early days of the Church.

For instance, the Bible tells us in Acts 6:3-6 that the apostles laid hands on a group of men who were to become deacons in the first church.

Wherefore, brethren, look ye out among you seven men of honest report, full of the Holy Ghost and wisdom, whom we may appoint over this business. But we will give ourselves continually to prayer, and to the ministry of the word. And the saying pleased the whole multitude: and they chose Stephen, a man full of faith and of the Holy Ghost, and Philip, and Prochorus, and Nicanor, and Timon, and Parmenas, and Nicolas a proselyte of Antioch: whom they set before the apostles: and when they had prayed, they laid their hands on them.

Notice that it *doesn't* say the apostles just prayed and acknowledged the men who were to take these positions. The apostles knew that in order for these men to be spiritually equipped and to receive the power to do their jobs, the apostles had to lay *their hands* on them. It was through the laying on of hands that a divine transfer of spiritual goods would take place. And in that instant when the apostles laid hands on these men, all the spiritual equipment they needed to be deacons was imparted to them.

So the apostles, who had been taught by Jesus, now continued in the pattern of their Master. They understood that through the laying on of hands, spiritual power would be imparted. They knew it wasn't enough to pray for them; they had to get their hands on them.

Then in Acts 13:1-3 (*NKJV*), we have the account of the ordination of Barnabas and Saul into apostolic ministry.

Now in the church that was at Antioch there were certain prophets and teachers: Barnabas, Simeon who was called Niger, Lucius of Cyrene, Manaen who had been brought up with Herod the tetrarch, and Saul. As they ministered to the Lord and fasted, the Holy Spirit said, "Now separate to Me Barnabas and Saul for the work to which I have called them." Then, having fasted and prayed, and laid hands on them, they sent them away.

The prophets and teachers in the Antioch church knew it was essential to get *their hands* on the two men God had called to fulfill a strategic assignment. They understood that through the laying on of hands, there would be a transfer to Barnabas and Saul of God's calling, anointing, gifting, and authority. And as the ministers laid their hands on the two men, the apostolic call was recognized, spiritual power was imparted, and special gifts needed for their calling were suddenly activated in the two men. All of that came through the laying on of hands.

In the same way, God's spiritual blessings can be transferred through the hands of believers to others today according to His leading and His purposes. As has been true through the centuries, the hands of God's chosen people are the instruments He has always chosen to use.

We see the laying on of hands demonstrated again in Acts 8:14-17. Philip had gone to Samaria to preach Christ to the people who lived there. This passage tells us what happened when Peter and John traveled to Samaria to join Philip:

Now when the apostles which were at Jerusalem heard that Samaria had received the word of God, they sent unto them Peter and John who, when they had come down, prayed for them, that they might receive the Holy Spirit. (For as yet he was fallen upon none of them: they were only baptized in

the name of the Lord Jesus.) Then they laid their hands on them, and they received the Holy Spirit.

The apostles prayed for the people to be filled with the Holy Spirit, but the people didn't receive until the apostles laid *their hands* on them. When that happened, a transfer of God's power took place, and at that moment, the people were baptized in the Holy Spirit. This experience of laying on of hands caused power to be visibly demonstrated in some way. In fact, a man named Simon the sorcerer was present, and whatever was happening that he witnessed caused him to covet the power that caused such a manifestation!

> And when Simon saw that through laying on of the apostles' hands the Holy Ghost was given, he offered them money, saying, Give me also this power, that on whomsoever I lay hands, he may receive the Holy Ghost.
>
> Acts 8:18,19

Notice it says, "And when Simon saw that through laying on of the apostles' hands…." There was something divine, something powerful happening that Simon could *see*, and it was the result of the divine impartation taking place as the apostles laid their hands on the people.

There was something divine,
something powerful happening that Simon could *see*,
and it was the result of the divine impartation
taking place as the apostles laid their hands
on the people.

Then in Acts 9:17 and 18, we have the powerful account of Saul of Tarsus himself (later to be called the apostle Paul). By the Lord's command, Ananias came to the house where Saul was staying. When Ananias entered the house, he knew he had to get his hands on Saul as quickly as he could. The Lord had told Ananias that it was through the laying on of *his hands* that Saul's eyes would be opened and he would be filled with the Holy Spirit.

Later in Acts 19:1-7, we have the account of the apostle Paul coming into upper Ephesus, where he found a group of men who had never heard about Jesus. The Bible says Paul preached Christ to them, and then it relates what transpired afterward: "When they heard this, they were baptized in the name of the Lord Jesus. And when Paul had laid *his hands* on them…" (vv. 5,6).

Even the legendary apostle Paul understood that he needed to get *his hands* on these new believers. And when Paul laid his hands on them, "…the Holy Ghost came on them; and they spoke with tongues, and prophesied." That supernatural event only occurred when Paul laid his hands on them.

THE LAYING ON OF HANDS
IN THE EPISTLES

Then in the New Testament epistles, we find some very key verses along this line. For example, in First Timothy 4:14 (*NKJV*), Paul wrote to Timothy: "Do not neglect the gift that is in you, which was given to you by prophecy with the laying on of the hands of the eldership." Paul in effect was saying to Timothy, "The gift that is in you was passed on to you through *hands.*" And Paul wrote down *whose* hands were laid on Timothy in his second epistle to the younger minister: "Wherefore I put thee in remembrance that thou stir up the gift of God, which is in thee by the putting on of *my* hands" (2 Timothy 1:6).

Paul understood that through *his hands*, spiritual gifts had passed into Timothy's life. Paul was so convinced of the importance of the laying on of hands that in Romans 1:11, he wrote to the Roman congregation and said, "For I long to see you, that I may impart unto you some spiritual gift, to the end ye may be established." Paul fully understood that he physically needed to be with them so he could lay *his hands* on them, and he was confident that through his hands they would receive a divine impartation. He was actually saying, *"That I may impart spiritual gifts unto you through my hands."*

YOUR HANDS ARE GOD'S INSTRUMENTS

So from the beginning to the end of Scripture, we find the importance of this doctrine of the laying on of hands. A particularly key scripture that highlights its significance is found in Mark 16:18. There we find Christ's command to *all* believers when He said, "…They [believers] shall lay hands on the sick, and they [the sick] shall recover." This means that every single believer is ordained by God to use his or her hands to deliver His power and blessing to someone else. This also means that a primary reason we don't see more supernatural activity is that God's people aren't using their hands.

Jesus Himself tells you, "Your hands are instruments for My power!" Friend, God wants to use *your* hands. Through your hands, He stands ready to impart His blessing, power, healing, and deliverance to others. You simply must yield by faith and obey His command to lay hands on those who need His touch as His Spirit leads you. If you'll get your hands out of your pockets and start laying them on people, you'll begin to see supernatural activity, because God works through the laying on of hands.

> If you'll get your hands out of your pockets
> and start laying them on people, you'll begin
> to see supernatural activity, because God
> works through the laying on of hands.

When you yield your hands for God to use them as His instruments, you will be amazed at the opportunities that come your way to transfer His blessings to others. Your hands may be used to impart the baptism in the Holy Spirit, healing to the sick, deliverance to the oppressed, an increase of financial blessing, anointings to carry out special tasks, or any of God's many other spiritual blessings that He's so eager to bestow upon those who will receive in faith.

GOD HAS TO HAVE YOUR HANDS

You may be one of those who has said, "I wonder why we don't see more signs and wonders in this modern day." But are you using *your* hands to lay hands on the sick? If you will determine to obey Jesus' command and begin to lay hands on the sick more, you will see more of God's power demonstrated and more healings manifested, because God works through hands.

You can see why this is a central doctrine of the Church and why it's such a crucial doctrine for you to understand, embrace, and *act on*. God desires power to be demonstrated in the Church, and He wants to use *you*. But in order to do that, He has to have your hands. That's just the way it is in God's Kingdom. His power is most often transferred through the laying on of hands.

So take one more look at your hands. Give yourself a moment to realize with fresh understanding that they are more than just hands — *they are instruments of God.* They may look like hands to you, but your hands are actually conduits through which all kinds of spiritual goods are meant to be transferred to other people. And as you lay hands on others by the leading of the Holy Spirit, you will begin to regularly see supernatural evidence of God's power and blessing manifested in people's lives because of your obedience.

Take one more look at your hands.
Give yourself a moment to realize
with fresh understanding that
they are more than just hands —
they are instruments of God.

There is one last point I want to share with you about this wonderful doctrine of the laying on of hands. *The prominence God gives this doctrine right in the very center of these other foundational doctrines shows us how interested He is in the personal touch.*

God wants to touch us with His hand, and He requires us to touch other people with *our* hands so that they can be ministered to and changed. Praise God for media ministry, but nothing will ever take the place of the human touch! God in His wisdom made it that way so we would have to be connected to one another to experience His fullness on the earth.

PRAYER TO LAY THE FOUNDATION OF THE LAYING ON OF HANDS

Father, today I recognize that my hands are Your instruments. You want to deliver Your gifts, Your power, Your healing, and Your deliverance through my hands to bless other people and to meet their needs. Today I give You my hands afresh as instruments and conduits for Your goodness to flow through me to others. I pray that through the laying on of hands, I will see a great increase of Your supernatural activity through me to bless many people's lives. In Jesus' name, amen.

THINK ABOUT IT

Hands are God's instruments. Throughout the Scriptures, we find that wisdom, healing, blessing, and spiritual gifts were among the impartations released into people's lives through the laying on of hands. The expression of this operation might be recognized more notably when ministers pray for people. But Jesus made it clear that one of the supernatural signs that follows all believers is they will lay hands on the sick and the sick will recover (*see* Mark 16:18).

Have you ever exercised the laying on of hands or been the recipient of hands laid on you? What was the result? God wants to demonstrate His power through His Church, and He wants to use your hands to heal the sick, deliver the oppressed, and impart blessings to those who will receive by faith. Are you willing to be a channel of His power? Can you identify some opportunities in your life outside of a church setting where you can yield yourself to God for His miracle power to be transferred to others through your hands?

The prominence God gives the doctrine of the laying on of hands reveals the value God places upon the personal touch. God formed us with His hand, and He wants to touch us with His hand. God also desires us to make meaningful contact with other people so they can be blessed and changed by His love and power flowing through us.

From the Old Testament into the New, each time the phrase "the hand of the Lord" is used, it depicts a moment when God's hand supernaturally came upon a person or a group to impart power or abilities to perform His purposes. How do you engage this powerful doctrine in your own life? Are you giving God access to others through you? Are you a "hands on" kind of person who prays for and blesses your family members regularly? Do you pray for the sick wherever you encounter them? Are you actively making disciples for Jesus Christ — laying hands on them to impart blessing or to activate spiritual gifts within them? If not, why not? That is something for you to think about!

Now that you have studied what the Bible teaches about the foundational doctrine of the laying on of hands, can you say with conviction that this doctrine is acknowledged and demonstrated in your life? If yes, in what ways? If not, what is your action plan to actively put this doctrine into operation in your life on a regular basis to bless others and bring honor to God?

7

THE DOCTRINE OF THE RESURRECTION OF THE DEAD

When I was 12 years old, my father said to me, "Rick, it's time for you to learn what it means to work. You're old enough to understand what it means to pay bills and make money. You need to get a job."

I asked my dad, "Where am I going to get a job?"

My father was ready with an answer. He said, "Go to the cemetery and apply for a job."

In obedience, I did exactly what my father asked me to do. I remember the day I made my way up the street to the cemetery, walked through the cemetery gate, into the midst of all the graves, and knocked on the door of the administrator's office. I told the cemetery director, "I'm here to apply for a job" — and he hired me!

I worked at the cemetery for two years. Every day after school, I would leave the school and walk directly to the cemetery, where I'd mow the grass on the graves; edge the grass around the tombstones; and collect dead flowers that people left on the graves. I'd even help in digging graves and burying the dead. For that two-year period of my life, I lived and worked among the dead every afternoon after school.

That experience was a very good one at that young stage of my life. Working among the dead made me think about life and realize that, no matter how long a person lives, life doesn't last very long. It was part of the Lord's training to prepare me for ministry.

In those two years, I had many experiences with grieving families while I worked at that cemetery. One thing that deeply impacted me was the difference between believing and unbelieving families at the time of death. When a Christian family buried a loved one who had been a believer, I noted that they were full of faith and had a very limited amount of sorrow. In fact, they often sang and found things to laugh and joke about with each other as they shared memories of their deceased loved one. It was evident that they had a sense of victory based in their faith that physical death is not the final word.

But when I encountered an unsaved family who were burying an unsaved loved one, it was a very different story and tragic to observe. For those who had no faith in the power of Jesus' death and resurrection, I saw such hopelessness because for them, the grave seemed so final. They were engulfed in sorrow because they had no hope of a resurrection. This stark difference between those who have faith and those who are devoid of faith was deeply instilled in me during that time of working in the cemetery as a young teenager.

Years later after Denise and I got married and I became an associate pastor, the senior pastor who was training me for the ministry said, "Rick, you need to learn how to conduct a funeral." With that, he sent me to officiate at my first funeral — and it was for an unsaved man from an unsaved family.

This man had died in his sixties after living an ungodly life. All his family members were also unsaved, among whom was his mother, a woman in her eighties. At the end of the funeral, the casket was opened so the family could walk by and pay their last respects to the dead (as is often the custom in the United States). When the mother walked by the casket, she was so overwhelmed with grief that she did something that took everyone off guard. Before anyone knew what was happening, she literally crawled into that casket!

Have you ever been to a funeral where someone crawled into the casket with the corpse of the dead person? Now just imagine what that might be like if it was the first funeral you'd ever officiated!

There I was with a grieving woman inside the casket lying on the deceased at my first funeral! Not only that, but while the mother was in the casket on top of her dead son, she was beating him on the chest and crying, "Don't you leave me! Don't you leave me!" Then she grabbed the lapels of his jacket and began to shake him, shouting, "Speak to me. Speak to me! *How dare you leave me!*"

The ushers had to gently pull that elderly woman out of the casket and escort her out of that room with her screaming all the way. It's quite a vivid memory for me even today!

But the woman was simply devoid of hope — and it wasn't just the mother of the man who had died. Grief and hopelessness were engulfing *all* his family members, because none of them were believers.

But as for us, we *are* believers, and we *do* have hope. For us, there is a future resurrection! And according to Hebrews 6:2, the resurrection of the dead is a central and fundamental doctrine of our faith.

We can certainly see why this would be true in the Early Church. Especially during the time when the book of Hebrews was being written, believers were being killed for their faith. They were literally giving their lives for Christ, and the hope of a future resurrection was central to their faith. It is also especially true for those of us who are part of this last-days generation of believers. The world is growing darker, and we're having to navigate the many challenges of this end-time season we have entered into. But through it all, we have a blessed hope! The resurrected Christ is returning soon for His Church!

DEATH HAS NO STING!

When my father died, I remember looking at his body lying in the casket. Although I deeply loved my father, I was not gripped with a sense of sorrow because I know what the Bible says about those who die in Christ.

First, I knew that the body lying in the casket was not my father — it was just the vessel he had lived in during his lifetime. According to Second Corinthians 5:8, my father was already in the presence of the Lord. So as I stood there, I thought, *This is the last time I'll see my father's body. The next time I see him, he is going to be completely different and so wonderful!* I knew that I knew that although my father's body had been sown in weakness, as the Bible says, he would be raised in power (*see* 1 Corinthians 15:43). One day in the future, he and I, along with all of our family, will have a glorious reunion in Heaven!

This is an amazing truth that is absolutely foundational to our faith, for our faith is securely rooted in a firm belief in the resurrection of the dead. The Bible tells us clearly that because of Christ's resurrection and our own future resurrection, the sting has been taken out of death (*see* 1 Corinthians 15:55). Death is indeed an enemy (*see* 1 Corinthians 15:26), but because of Christ's resurrection and His promise of our own resurrection, death is *not* something we need to fear. Oh, how we need to get a revelation of this truth and build it strong into the foundation of our faith in Christ!

Death is indeed an enemy
but because of Christ's resurrection
and His promise of our own resurrection,
death is *not* something we need to fear.

Perhaps you can see a little more clearly why the resurrection of the dead was included in the list of elementary doctrines in Hebrews 6:1,2 and why it must be such a strong component of our spiritual foundation. So let's dig deeper to discover more about this fundamental doctrine. As we do, I pray the revelation of Christ's resurrection power gets firmly planted in your heart so that you are better equipped to build a solid "high-rise" structure called *your life of faith in God* as you move forward.

WHAT DOES 'RESURRECTION' MEAN?

The Church of the Holy Sepulcher in Jerusalem houses the tomb where Jesus was buried and from which He was resurrected. Over the past 2,000 years, Christians have surrounded that tomb with a great deal of ornamentation. But behind that ornate façade, there is an ancient tomb that is empty for one reason only — *because Jesus was raised from the dead.*

Our belief in Jesus' resurrection is part of the bedrock of our faith. In fact, if we don't believe in Christ's resurrection and our own future resurrection, we really don't have anything to base our faith on (*see* 1 Corinthians 15:14). This is confirmed by the fact that the resurrection from the dead is included in this list of fundamental doctrines in Hebrews 6. That means it is a part of the foundation that upholds everything else we believe, and it is critical for us to understand it.

So what does the Bible teach about the resurrection of the dead? When I have visited the Church of the Holy Sepulcher in Jerusalem in times past, that was one question I thought about a great deal.

The word translated "resurrection" throughout the New Testament is the compound Greek word *anastasis.* The word *ana* means *to repeat something* or *to do it again.* The word *stasis* is the Greek word that simply means *to stand.* When you compound the two words, the new word means *to stand again, to stand upright,* or *to be raised from the dead.*

This is the very meaning of "resurrection" as Jesus used it in John 11:25 when He said, "I am the Resurrection and the Life."

Jesus said unto her, I am the resurrection, and the life: he that believeth in me, though he were dead, yet shall he live.

In this particular case in John 11, Jesus was speaking about a physical resurrection. But Jesus' resurrection power is not limited to just the physical realm. Jesus *is anastasis*! That means if you have been knocked down by life — if your emotions have been crushed, if your finances have been negatively impacted, if you're down in *any* area of your life — the resurrection power of Jesus can cause you to stand up again!

Jesus said to Martha, "I am the *Resurrection* and the Life" (*see* John 11:25). That word "resurrection" is that Greek word *anastasis*. It was the equivalent of saying, *"I am stand-again power! If you've been knocked flat — even if you're dead — I have the power to put you on your feet again! I am the Power who causes people to stand up again. I am the Power who will raise you back to life!"*

If you have been knocked down by life —
if your emotions have been crushed,
if your finances have been negatively impacted,
if you're down in *any* area of your life —
the resurrection power of Jesus
can cause you to stand up again!

It is glorious news to know that Jesus will one day raise you from the dead. But you also need to know that if you've been knocked flat by life, Jesus is your Resurrection *right now*! As you embrace Him and His grace, He'll put you on your feet again. He is *anastasis*. He *is* Resurrection itself. He *is* "stand-up power"! That one thought is enough to get you moving toward the victory that is ahead of you. His power is sufficient to raise you up *to stand strong* in the midst of every battle!

Our Sure Guarantee

The apostle Paul talked about the importance of the Resurrection in First Corinthians 15:19,20. This is a very important passage of Scripture on this subject.

If in this life only we have hope in Christ, we are of all men most miserable. But now is Christ risen from the dead, and become the firstfruits of them that slept.

Paul was categorically stating that *Jesus Christ's resurrection from the dead is the guarantee that we also will be raised from the dead.* Christ was the *first fruits*; His resurrection is the promise that another harvest of resurrections will follow after Him.

When you study the Old Testament, you find three concrete examples of resurrection — of people who were raised from the dead (*see* 1 Kings 17:17-22; 2 Kings 4:32-35; 2 Kings 13:20,21). However, there are many more than just the three specifically enumerated in the Old Testament because in Hebrews 11:35, it says that there were *many* women who received their dead back to life again. We can therefore conclude that in addition to the three concrete examples, other instances of people being raised from the dead also occurred during Old Testament times.

In the earthly ministry of Jesus, three people are recorded as raised from the dead (*see* Luke 7:11-15; Luke 8:41,42,49-55; John 11:1-44). But there were actually more than that during the time He was still on the earth, because Matthew 27:52 (*NKJV*) says that as Jesus yielded up His spirit on the Cross, the earth quaked, "...and the graves were opened; and many bodies of the saints who had fallen asleep were raised."

Then in the book of Acts, if we count the apostle Paul himself after he was stoned in Lystra, there are again three concrete examples of people who were raised from the dead in the days of the Early Church (*see* Acts 9:36-41; 14:19,20; 20:9,10).

But think of this for a moment: All of those people who were raised from the dead under the Old and New Covenants eventually died again. Their resurrections were temporary. They were raised, and then they lived a normal life — and eventually, all of them died again.

There is only one resurrection of One who did *not* die again, and that is the resurrection of Jesus Christ. If there had never been a resurrection of Christ from the dead, Jesus' sacrificial death on the Cross never could have brought the life of God to you and me. But Christ *was* raised from the dead, having tasted death for all men (*see* Hebrews 2:9). He seized the keys of hell and the grave (*see* Revelation 1:18). He conquered death once and for all (*see* Romans 6:10; 2 Timothy 1:10)! And Christ never died again — nor will He *ever* die again. This is such an amazing truth for us to fully grasp!

Jesus Christ's resurrection from the dead is the guarantee that we also will be raised from the dead.

In First Corinthians 15:3 and 4, the apostle Paul stated this foundational principle that we're focusing on with perfect clarity: "For I delivered unto you first of all that which I also received, how that Christ died for our sins according to the scriptures. And that he was buried, and that he rose again the third day according to the scriptures."

This is truly the cornerstone of our faith. Someone may ask, "Isn't the Cross the cornerstone?" But thousands and thousands of people were crucified over the years. Only One was raised from the dead. If Jesus had died but there had been no resurrection, we would not have a living faith. *It is His resurrection that is truly the cornerstone of our faith.*

And it's important to understand that after the resurrection, the reality of that event was verified multiple times. Jesus' resurrection was affirmed when He appeared ten different times to different individuals and groups of people.

1. He appeared to Mary Magdalene (*see* Mark 16:9; John 20: 11-18).

2. He appeared to other women (*see* Matthew 28:9,10; Luke 23:55 – 24:10).

3. He appeared to Peter (*see* Luke 24:34; 1 Corinthians 15:5).

4. He appeared to the two disciples on the road to Emmaus (*see* Luke 24:13-33).

5. He appeared to ten of the disciples all at once (*see* John 20:19,20).

6. He appeared to 11 disciples eight days later (*see* Matthew 28:16,17; John 20:26).

7. He appeared to seven disciples at the Sea of Tiberius (*see* John 21:1-25).

8. On one occasion, Jesus appeared to 500 people. They all saw Him. In fact, when Paul wrote about that, he said many of them were still alive and could still testify about it at the time of his writing (*see* 1 Corinthians 15:6).

9. He appeared to James, the Lord's brother (*see* 1 Corinthians 15:7).

10. At the moment of His ascension, He had appeared to the 11 apostles (*see* Acts 1:6-11).

If Jesus had died but there had been no resurrection, we would not have a living faith.

Jesus appeared over and over and over again after His resurrection. This is most likely not the full list because in Acts 1:3, Luke wrote, "...He shewed himself alive after his passion by many infallible proofs, being seen of them forty days...." This word "them," of course, is plural. It's talking about multiple appearances and a vast number of people who saw Him — and it was proof to all that Jesus had indeed risen from the dead.

THREE FUTURE RESURRECTIONS FOR TWO GROUPS OF PEOPLE

In John 5:28 and 29, Jesus said that there would be separate resurrections in the future for two different groups of people.

...The hour is coming, in the which all that are in the graves shall hear his voice, and shall come forth; they that have

done good, unto the resurrection of life; and they that have done evil, unto the resurrection of damnation.

There is going to be a resurrection for those who are righteous — in other words, for those who are saved by their faith in the redemptive work of Jesus. But Jesus also told us of another resurrection that would occur for those who have done evil. He called it "the resurrection of damnation."

This truth about the coming resurrections for two groups of people is taught throughout Scripture. But when will these future resurrections take place? We're going to go through Scripture point by point to answer that question and prove how we can know this to be true.

First, there will be a resurrection for the *saved.* This resurrection will occur simultaneously with what is commonly called "the rapture of the Church." That is the first resurrection, which will actually happen in the near future.

When Jesus comes for the Church, if you and I have already died, we will be raised from the dead to meet the Lord first in the air. Everyone who has died in Christ will be raised from the dead at the moment of the Rapture. And if we are still alive on the earth, we will be next — caught up in the air to meet the Lord (*see* 1 Thessalonians 4:14-17).

Second, there is another resurrection for the righteous in Christ beyond the Rapture. This resurrection will occur at the end of the Tribulation, and it will be for those who died as martyrs for their faith in Christ during the Tribulation. The Bible tells us that at the end of the Tribulation, they will be raised from the dead (*see* Revelation 20:4-6).

Third, there is a final resurrection of the dead. This final resurrection will be for the *unrighteous* — those who never received Jesus as their Savior and Lord. It's what Jesus called a "resurrection unto damnation." This resurrection will occur at the very end of the Millennial reign of Christ on the earth (*see* Revelation 20:4,6), just before the Great White Throne Judgment (*see* Revelation 20:11-15). (We will deal with that subject in the next chapter when we talk about the doctrine of eternal judgment.)

Everyone who has died in Christ will be raised
from the dead at the moment of the Rapture. And if
we are still alive on the earth, we will be next —
caught up in the air to meet the Lord.

So there are three separate resurrections that will occur in the future — two for the righteous and one for the unrighteous. Let's look at each of these more closely one by one.

THE FIRST RESURRECTION: THE RAPTURE OF THE CHURCH

The first resurrection will happen simultaneously with the rapture of the Church. The apostle Paul wrote about this in First Thessalonians 4:14-17.

For if we believe that Jesus died and rose again, even so them also which sleep in Jesus will God bring with him. For this we say unto you by the word of the Lord, that we which are alive and remain unto the coming of the Lord shall not prevent them which are asleep. For the Lord himself shall descend from heaven with a shout, with the voice

of the archangel, and with the trump of God: and the dead in Christ shall rise first: Then we which are alive and remain shall be caught up together with them in the clouds, to meet the Lord in the air: and so shall we ever be with the Lord.

Notice what it says in verse 16: "…And the dead in Christ shall rise first." Here, then, is the declaration of the resurrection of the righteous at the moment of the Rapture. The dead will be raised first; then we who are alive on the earth at that time will be "…caught up together with them in the clouds, to meet the Lord in the air: and so shall we ever be with the Lord" (v. 17). That is the moment we call the Rapture.

First Thessalonians 4:18 goes on to say, "Wherefore comfort one another with these words." This knowledge is intended to comfort and strengthen God's people — that there is a future resurrection of the righteous when Jesus Christ comes again to receive His Church.

In First Corinthians 15:51-53 (*NKJV*), Paul affirmed again this resurrection of the righteous that will happen at the moment of the Rapture:

Behold, I tell you a mystery: We shall not all sleep, but we shall all be changed — in a moment, in the twinkling of an eye, at the last trumpet. For the trumpet will sound, and the dead will be raised incorruptible, and we shall be changed. For this corruptible must put on incorruption, and this mortal must put on immortality.

In Philippians 3:20,21 (*NKJV*), Paul once more referred to this first resurrection:

For our citizenship is in heaven, from which we also eagerly wait for the Savior, the Lord Jesus Christ, who will transform

our lowly body that it may be conformed to His glorious body, according to the working by which He is able even to subdue all things to Himself.

Believers of every generation have been waiting for Jesus to return — anticipating the rapture of the Church. But Paul went on to tell us what will happen simultaneously with that event. When the righteous are resurrected, they are going to receive new, glorified, resurrected bodies that will be like Jesus' resurrected body.

Consider what we know about Jesus' body after His resurrection. He could effortlessly move from one place to another. He could walk through walls (*see* John 20:19). He could do things that He couldn't have done in His natural body. And how do we receive our resurrected bodies? Either by being raised from the dead or by being raptured at the sound of Heaven's trumpet. Both categories of believers will instantaneously receive the same glorified bodies.

In our resurrected bodies, there will be no sickness, no infirmity, no problems. We will be everything we always wished we could be — because we will be just like Jesus.

In our resurrected bodies, there will be no sickness, no infirmity, no problems. We will be everything we always wished we could be — because we will be just like Jesus.

What a day it will be when the dead, corruptible bodies of those who have died in Christ become miraculously incorruptible!

And we who are alive and are mortal — in the *twinkling* of an eye — will change and put on immortality.

THE SECOND RESURRECTION:
THE RESURRECTION OF THE RIGHTEOUS

The Bible is very clear about this *first resurrection* of the righteous that occurs with the Rapture. But Scripture also reveals that there will be a *second resurrection* of the righteous, which occurs at the end of the Tribulation. This future event is found in Revelation 20:4,5.

> **And I saw thrones, and they sat upon them, and judgment was given unto them: and I saw the souls of them that were beheaded for the witness of Jesus, and for the word of God, and which had not worshipped the beast, neither his image, neither had received his mark upon their foreheads, or in their hands; and they lived and reigned with Christ a thousand years. But the rest of the dead lived not again until the thousand years were finished. This is the first resurrection.**

In this verse, we find two resurrections. First, the second resurrection of the righteous at the end of the Tribulation. Then verse 5 goes on to say, "…The rest of the dead lived not again [or they were not raised to life again] until the thousand years were finished" — in other words, just before the Great White Throne Judgment. We'll talk about this *third resurrection* next.

THE THIRD RESURRECTION:
THE RESURRECTION OF THE UNRIGHTEOUS

Let's look again at Revelation 20:5: "But the rest of the dead lived not again until the end of the thousand years were finished."

Who are "the rest of the dead" referred to here? By the end of the Tribulation, everyone who has died in faith will have already been resurrected, and all the righteous will be in Heaven to partake of the Marriage Supper of the Lamb and to stand before the Judgment Seat of Christ to receive rewards (*see* 2 Corinthians 5:9-10). And when Jesus returns to set up the Millennial reign on the earth, the righteous will come with Him to form the government of His Kingdom on the earth for a thousand years. This is what the Bible tells us.

Then at the very end of the Millennial reign of Christ, the *rest* of the dead — the *unrighteous* who did not die in faith — will be summoned out of their graves. Revelation 20:12-15 tells us about this third and final resurrection:

And I saw the dead, small and great, stand before God; and the books were opened: and another book was opened, which is the book of life: and the dead were judged out of those things which were written in the books, according to their works. And the sea gave up the dead which were in it; and death and hell delivered up the dead which were in them: and they were judged every man according to their works. And death and hell were cast into the lake of fire. This is the second death. And whosoever was not found written in the book of life was cast into the lake of fire.

In this *final* resurrection, the unsaved will be summoned to be judged before the Great White Throne Judgment. (Those who are in Christ will *not* stand before the Great White Throne for judgment.) The Bible clearly teaches that unsaved people are destined for the fire of an eternal hell, and we will discuss this further in the next chapter. I realize it is no longer considered culturally correct to say that unsaved people will go to hell, but this is what the Bible teaches, and we are obligated to speak the truth about it.

It's crucial that we understand that there is a future judgment of the unsaved — because none of us wants anyone to experience that. The revelation of this truth will ignite our hearts to obey God more fully regarding our responsibility as believers. We are to share the saving news of Jesus Christ and to ask the Holy Spirit to open the eyes of the spiritually blind so they can come to Christ and avoid this final judgment that will happen at the end of the Millennial reign.

We need to know what the Bible says about the resurrection of the dead, because it is a foundational doctrine to our faith. It's crucial for us to understand that regardless of whether people have accepted or rejected Jesus Christ, every person who has ever lived is going to be raised in one of the three resurrections to come.

It is no longer considered culturally correct to say
that unsaved people will go to hell, but this
is what the Bible teaches, and we
are obligated to speak the truth about it.

As for us, it's certain that if Jesus tarries His coming, there will be a funeral in our future. And if there's a funeral in our future, it is essential for us to confidently know what lies *beyond* our funeral or the time of our death — the time of our passing from this earth. Thank God for the anchor of hope He has given us — that for those of us who die in Christ, a glorious resurrection awaits! Jesus was the "first fruits" and the divine Guarantee that there would be a great harvest of His people resurrected after Him. And the hope of that glorious event that lies ahead in the not-too-distant future includes you and me!

PRAYER TO LAY THE FOUNDATION
OF THE RESURRECTION OF THE DEAD

Father, I thank You for Your Word, and for the assurance both for living and for dying that I have as Your child. I thank You that Jesus was raised as the "first fruits" and that I can rest peacefully in the knowledge that I will follow in His resurrection on that day when all Your people rise to meet Him in the air.

What a blessed hope that is to look forward to! I am so thankful, and I purpose to bring as many people with me as I can in that first resurrection by faithfully sharing the Good News of Jesus at every opportunity. In Jesus' name, amen.

THINK ABOUT IT

The bedrock of our Christian faith is based on the resurrection of Jesus Christ. Paul shares what he received by revelation of the Spirit in First Thessalonians 4:13-17 — that those who die in the Lord shall be resurrected to return with Him when He establishes His Millennial reign on earth.

For this cause, we do not sorrow or grieve as those who do not have this hope when we have loved ones who die in the Lord. We know that their spirits are eternally with the Lord. And although their bodies may have been sown in weakness, as the Bible says, they will be raised in power (*see* 1 Corinthians 15:43). That promise of resurrection from the dead is what the apostle Paul explained when he said, "The corruptible must put on incorruption." He then boldly proclaimed, "O death, where is your sting? O grave, where is your victory?" (*see* 1 Corinthians 15:51-55).

Do you know someone who has experienced the passing of a loved one who died in the Lord, yet that bereaved person struggles to recover from grief? How can you reach out to that person to help him derive comfort by becoming established in this foundational doctrine so that his perspective can shift from the pain of a natural loss to the joy of spiritual gain in Christ?

Resurrection power is not limited to just the physical realm. Think about it: Have you been knocked down by life in any way?

Have your emotions been crushed by the end of a relationship, an association, or even of a marriage that you thought would last forever? Have your finances been hit so that you do not know how you can recover? Have you been knocked down and left for dead, so to speak, in any area of your life? As you pursue a greater revelation of the resurrection power of Jesus Christ, that power will raise you up and cause you to live again in that area.

Three separate resurrections will occur in the future — two for the righteous and one for the unrighteous. The Bible teaches these truths, and it is crucial that we understand that hell is a real place — whether it is popular or a culturally correct concept or not. How people respond to the saving knowledge of Jesus Christ before they die — in this life — will determine their resurrection and eternal destination.

Are you actively and compassionately preparing others (and yourself!) to face eternity? Are you preaching the complete truth of the Gospel to let people know there is a Heaven to gain and a hell to shun? When you stand before Jesus to receive your reward, will it include a soulwinner's crown, or will He ask you why you didn't give people an opportunity to avoid hell and to join Him in Heaven? You will have to give an account. Are you doing all you can to spread the Gospel and to help others do likewise? Think about it. *Jesus is coming soon!*

8

THE DOCTRINE
OF ETERNAL JUDGMENT

We've come to the last in the list of foundational doctrines found in Hebrews 6:1,2 that we need for our lives. In this chapter, I believe you're going to gain a brand-new understanding of what the Bible calls "eternal judgment." This doctrine, like the other five we have looked at, describes one of the *starting points* in the ABCs of our faith. Every Christian needs to know this doctrine, as it is one of the essential doctrines of the Christian faith.

As we've seen, Hebrews 6:1 starts out by saying we are not to get stuck in the elementary principles of the faith, but we are to grow up and move on to deeper understanding of the truths of God's Word. There's so much more He wants to reveal to us. But a child doesn't go to the twelfth grade until first he has passed the first, second, and third grades, and so on.

This is God's intention — that you keep growing, advancing, and going on unto perfection, or *maturity*, in Him. And these elementary doctrines are crucial for you to understand before you go on to learn other truths because they are so foundational to your faith.

Let's review the first five doctrines we've covered so far.

1. *Repentance from dead works:* You must understand what repentance *is* — and what repentance is *not*. You must know how to truly repent. This knowledge is foundational to your faith.

2. *Faith toward God:* We saw how this describes *a faith that rests wholly on Christ and not on anything else.* This is so important that it is essential for you to understand in order to be saved.

3. *The doctrines of baptisms:* There are three baptisms in the New Testament, and God wants you to have all three. One is absolutely essential to be saved — your baptism into the Body of Christ. The other two are central to your faith — water baptism and the baptism in the Holy Spirit. It is crucial for a strong spiritual foundation that you understand and receive all three.

4. *Laying on of hands:* We saw that the laying on of hands is a well-established, holy practice throughout Scripture. God uses human hands to impart power, gifts, healing, blessing, authority, and the infilling of the Holy Spirit. The laying on of hands is central to the power of God being operational in the Church.

5. *The resurrection of the dead:* The Bible teaches there are three resurrections that will take place in the future. In the

first resurrection, everyone who has died in Christ, along with those who are alive on earth, will be raised from the dead when the rapture of the Church takes place. A second resurrection will occur at the end of the Tribulation, when all those who received Christ and died as martyrs during the Tribulation will be raised from the dead. Finally, at the very end of the Millennial reign of Christ will come the third and final resurrection when the unsaved will be resurrected and summoned before God to give account for their lives. The Bible calls this the Great White Throne Judgment, which we will discuss more in-depth in this chapter.

THE GREAT WHITE THRONE JUDGMENT

Now let's move on to the final doctrine listed in Hebrews 6:1,2 — the doctrine of *eternal judgment.*

What is eternal judgment? Hebrews 6:2 says this subject is so important that we need to know what the Bible says about it as part of our essential spiritual foundation. In fact, this knowledge should be *set in stone* in our lives. Every person is going to face a future time of reckoning, so it is critical for us to know the kind of judgment we will face according to our choices during our time on the earth and how to correctly prepare for our personal time of reckoning before the Lord.

But let's begin with the judgment that awaits the unbelieving, unsaved, ungodly world. In the last chapter, we saw that there will be a resurrection of the unjust at the end of the Millennial reign. At the very end of Christ's thousand-year reign on the earth, the unsaved will be summoned forth from their graves to stand before the Great White Throne Judgment.

As I said in the last chapter, if you are a believer, you will *not* stand before the Great White Throne to be judged, because you are in Christ. The Great White Throne Judgment is only for the ungodly, or the unsaved. The Bible talks about this in Revelation 20:11-15.

> **And I saw a great white throne, and him that sat on it, from whose face the earth and the heaven fled away; and there was found no place for them. And I saw the dead, small and great, stand before God; and the books were opened: and another book was opened, which is the book of life: and the dead were judged out of those things which were written in the books, according to their works.**
>
> **And the sea gave up the dead which were in it; and death and hell delivered up the dead which were in them: and they were judged every man according to their works. And death and hell were cast into the lake of fire. This is the second death. And whosoever was not found written in the book of life was cast into the lake of fire.**

Every person is going to face
a future time of reckoning, so it is critical
for us to know the kind of judgment we will face
according to our choices during our time
on the earth and how to correctly prepare
for our personal time of reckoning
before the Lord.

Notice that in verse 12, it says, "And I saw the dead, small and great, stand before God...." That phrase "small and great" means *everyone, regardless of his or her status — all of those who died out of faith*. Verse 12 continues to say, "...The books were opened: and another Book was opened, which is the Book of Life."

Here we find that God is a Keeper of records and that there are books — *plural* — in Heaven. But notice there is one book called, "The Book of Life." That is a book that holds the names of all those who have put their faith in Jesus Christ. Remember how Jesus answered the apostles when they said, "Lord, we have authority over demons!" Jesus replied, "Don't rejoice about that; instead, rejoice that your names are written in Heaven" (*see* Luke 10:17-20). If a person is saved, his or her name is written in Heaven, and those whose names are found written in the Book of Life are going to go to Heaven.

Revelation 20:12 goes on to tell us what will happen to those whose names are *not* found in the Book of Life. They will be judged according to what is written about their works on the earth in the other books. Then in verse 15, it says, "And whosoever was not found written in the Book of Life was cast into the lake of fire." This is the eternal destiny of every person who dies without Christ.

As you read this passage of Scripture, you may be tempted to grieve about your loved ones who have already died without Christ. That is a true tragedy, but don't let the devil get you fixated on something that has already happened that you cannot change. What God wants you to do is to focus on everyone who is still alive and whom you can help lead into His Kingdom!

We each need to make the decision that we will do our utmost to make sure no one else goes to hell. That's why we must share the message of Jesus Christ at every opportunity and use the rest of our time on this earth to rescue as many people as we can so they will not stand before the Great White Throne Judgment that will surely take place at a future time.

We must share the message of Jesus Christ
at every opportunity and use the rest of our time
on this earth to rescue as many people as we can so they
will not stand before the Great White Throne Judgment
that will surely take place at a future time.

But remember — this Great White Throne Judgment is *not* for you and me *if* we are in Jesus Christ.

THE JUDGMENT SEAT OF CHRIST

There is another judgment for believers, which is called the Judgment Seat of Christ. This event is reserved for true believers, and it will occur after the rapture of the Church during the seven years of the Tribulation while we are in Heaven.

During that time in Heaven, two events will take place involving the redeemed: the Marriage Supper of the Lamb and the Judgment Seat of Christ. There are some misconceptions about this latter future event, many of which were caused by preachers who didn't gain an understanding of this doctrine in the ABCs of faith and therefore preached things that were incorrect. One common misconception is that "the Judgment Seat of Christ" will be a place and time when we will stand before Jesus to give account for the sins we committed in our lives. That's not what this Judgment Seat is about, as we will see in the pages to come.

When Denise and I were adolescents, each growing up in our respective churches, we were often terrified by preachers who said, "When you stand before the Judgment Seat of Christ, a movie is going to be projected that shows everything you ever did in your life. And in that moment, Christ, the angels, all your friends, all your neighbors — *everyone* will see every sin you committed and every mistake you ever made." I remember as a young person thinking to myself, *I do not want to see that movie.* I don't know about you, but I don't want a movie to ever be made about every wrong thing I did in my life!

But is that what the Bible actually says will happen? No, it isn't. Although some might think that's an effective way to scare people into living right, it is totally contrary to the teaching of Scripture. Why would God deal with us about sins that have been placed under the blood of Jesus? Romans 8:1 assures us, "There is therefore now no condemnation to them which are in Christ Jesus...." And First John 1:9 says God cleanses us from *all* unrighteousness when we repent and confess our sins to Him — just as if we never sinned.

When you stand before the Judgment Seat of Christ, it is not for the purpose of condemnation or of rehearsing every sin you ever committed. Furthermore, God is *not* going to deal with you about sins you have confessed and placed under the blood of Jesus. He will never bring up those sins to you again, not even at the Judgment Seat of Christ. He isn't going to say, "Excuse Me, but I'm going to reach into your past and extract from under the blood of Jesus every sin that has already been forgiven, and I'm going to deal with you about all those sins anyway." As we discussed in an earlier chapter, once your sin is placed under the blood of Jesus, *it is under the blood of Jesus forever.* If your sin has been confessed, repented of, and placed under the blood of Jesus, it means God has removed it as far as the east is from the west (*see* Ps. 103:12), and He will never deal with you about it in eternity, because that sin has become nonexistent in the mind of God.

Then what is the Judgment Seat of Christ actually about? It is the place where He will deal with us about what we did with our lives *after* we came to Christ. How willingly and how fully did we carry out what Jesus asked us to do? When we stand before the Judgment Seat of Christ, He will assess our obedience to Him after we received Him as our Savior and Lord. It will be a place of evaluation, and on the basis of that evaluation, rewards will be given and our position of service in the Millennial reign of Christ will be revealed.

God is *not* going to deal with you about sins
you have confessed and placed under the blood of Jesus.
He will never bring up those sins to you again,
not even at the Judgment Seat of Christ.

You see, *we are currently in a qualification period for the next age.* It's a mistake to think you are living only for right now, as if what you do right now is your goal. Certainly, achieving victories right now is a great goal, but our present level of obedience is qualifying us for a very long period of service in His Kingdom during the Millennial reign — and right on into eternity! Each of us who is in Christ is destined to enter this next age, and what happens at the Judgment Seat of Christ will determine whether we will be small or great.

We are currently in a qualification period for the next age. Our present level of obedience is qualifying us for a very long period of service in His Kingdom during the Millennial reign — and right on into eternity!

Remember that eternal judgment is a fundamental doctrine of Christ that is absolutely vital for you to understand. It is imperative that you know what the Bible teaches about the Judgment Seat of Christ. *Our current level of obedience in this present age is what determines our places of service and responsibility in the next age.*

WE WILL STAND WITHOUT SHAME BEFORE JESUS

But let's explore further what the Bible explicitly tells us about the Judgment Seat of Christ. The apostle Paul specifically referred to this future event twice in Scripture. The first instance is found in Romans 14:10,12 (*NKJV*): "…For we shall all stand before the judgment seat of God…. So then each of us shall give account of himself to God."

Notice that it says, "We shall all *stand*." The word "stand" comes from the Greek word *peristome*, which simply means *to stand*. It does *not* mean *to crawl* or *to grovel*!

When we will stand before the Judgment Seat of Christ, we will not be shamed for our past sin. The Judgment Seat of Christ is *not* a place of shame, nor is it a place of embarrassment. We're going to "stand" before Christ at that moment, and we will *not* grovel in His presence. We will *stand* before Him as those who are washed in His blood and robed in His righteousness.

It is interesting to note that in the original Greek of the New Testament, the word "judgment" does not appear in the Greek text at all. Instead, the Greek text uses the word *bema*. If you were going to translate the sentence correctly, it would say, "We are going to stand before the *bema* of God." This word *bema* is so very important that you must understand what it means.

The word *bema* is taken from the Isthmian Games — athletic games that were carried out in the ancient city of Isthmia in Greece. It was a biannual event in which athletes competed for a reward under the careful scrutiny of judges who watched to make sure every rule of the contest was obeyed. The Isthmian games were particularly famous for foot races. After the games concluded, the victors came before a platform that was called the *bema*. This was the place where the judge stood to place laurel crowns on the heads of those who had competed well and according to the rules. It was *not* a place where losers were whipped or condemned. Thus, the *bema* historically was a place of evaluation and designation.

> The Judgment Seat of Christ is *not* a place of shame, nor is it a place of embarrassment. We will *stand* before Him as those who are washed in His blood and robed in His righteousness.

By using the word *bema*, Paul in essence was saying that we are like competitors who are running a spiritual race. And just as victorious athletes of the Isthmian games appeared before the *bema* to receive a physical reward, one day we will be brought before Jesus Christ's *bema* — the platform where He will be standing — and there Christ will evaluate our various levels of obedience and will designate what kind of reward we will receive.

Just as the ancient Greeks' *bema* was not a seat of punishment for those who lost the contests, the *bema* of Christ is also not a place of punishment for us as believers. When we stand before Jesus, He is not going to whip us or castigate us for our failures. Instead, it will be a place of evaluation where Christ will weigh and assess our works, our efforts, and our faith. It will also be a place of designation where He will determine the kind of reward that should be given to us for what we did in obedience to His plan.

We Will Give Account of Our Lives to Jesus

This is the nature of the Judgment Seat of Christ, which is very different from any erroneous concept of this future event as a place of condemnation and judgment for us as believers. Where the Bible says we will give account of ourselves to God (*see* Romans 14:12), the words "give account" come from a Greek word that means *to give a factual report*. When we stand before the Lord, He will require us to give a factual report of what we did and what we did not do in regard to what He asked of us.

The *bema* of Christ is a place where we will not be able to escape the facts as Jesus reviews our level of obedience after we were born again and evaluates us on how well we truly ran our spiritual race. Did we do what He asked us to do? Did we complete our role in the "games of the Kingdom" during our time on the earth? A factual report is in my future — and it is in your future as well.

Paul wrote about this future event in Second Corinthians 5:10 when he said, "For we must all appear before the judgment seat of Christ; that every one may receive the things done in his body, according to that he hath done, whether it be good or bad." Let's look at some of the words in this verse.

First, Paul wrote, "We must all *appear*...." The word "appear" comes from the Greek word *phaneros*, which is the same Greek word that describes a *revealing* of some kind. This word *phaneros* also conveys the meaning of *making oneself fully known by removing all pretenses*. This means when we appear before Christ in the light of the *bema*, all disguises will evaporate and it will be a moment of great revealing regarding how we obeyed Christ after we were saved. There may have been negative things we were able to camouflage or hide from other people's eyes during our lifetime, but when we appear before Christ, the real story of our walk with God will be revealed. It will be a time when Jesus assesses our acts of obedience or our lack of obedience as a part of His evaluation process.

There may have been negative things we were able
to camouflage or hide from other people's eyes
during our lifetime, but when we appear before Christ,
the real story of our walk with God will be revealed.

The phrase translated "judgment seat" that Paul used in Second Corinthians 5:10 again is the Greek word *bema*. Once again, it refers to that future event when Jesus will evaluate the redeemed and designate the kind of reward that each is to receive. And notice that the Bible says "every one" will be evaluated. The words "every one" is a translation of the Greek word *hekastos*, which is an *all-inclusive* word that embraces every single believer.

There is no escaping this future event. *Every single one of us* who has received Jesus as our Savior and Lord is going to appear before the Judgment Seat of Christ to receive what is due to us according to what we have done in our walk with Him on the earth.

In fact, Paul said that at that moment, everyone will "receive" according to what is determined during that time of evaluation. The word "receive" is a translation of the Greek word *komidzo*, which means *to receive what a person has coming to him*. If a believer has worked hard and done his best to obey God's plan for his life, he will have a reward coming to him. If he *hasn't* worked very hard to obey God and do what He called him to do, he may not have much reward coming to him, even though he is saved and in Heaven. Paul made it clear that *every* believer will face this moment of evaluation regarding "the things done in the body" before the *bema* of Christ.

Our Works Will Be Made Manifest Before Jesus

In First Corinthians 3:10-15, without mentioning the *bema* seat specifically, Paul explained what is going to happen at this future event and exactly how we will be evaluated when we stand before Jesus.

> **According to the grace of God which is given unto me, as a wise masterbuilder, I have laid the foundation, and another buildeth thereon. But let every man take heed how he buildeth thereupon. For other foundation can no man lay than that is laid, which is Jesus Christ.**

Now if any man build upon this foundation gold, silver, precious stones, wood, hay, stubble; Every man's work shall be made manifest: for the day shall declare it, because it shall be revealed by fire; and the fire shall try every man's work of what sort it is.

If any man's work abide which he hath built thereupon, he shall receive a reward. If any man's work shall be burned, he shall suffer loss: but he himself shall be saved; yet so as by fire.

What you do with your life after the moment of salvation is your gift to God, and *that* is what is going to be evaluated at the *bema* of Christ.

Paul was again teaching about that future day of evaluation when we will be rewarded based on what we have built with our lives. Verse 13 states it this way: "Every man's work shall be made manifest." It emphatically does *not* say our *salvation* will be tested; it says that our *work* will be "made manifest."

This passage lets us know that a day is coming in the future when our level of obedience in life — whether we have truly done what God told us to do and with a right motivation — will be revealed. Verse 13 says it will be revealed "by fire," which carries the idea of *a scrutinizing test.* It describes a very thorough and intense examination that will occur when we stand before Christ. The verse goes on to say that time of evaluation will "try every man's work of what sort it is."

> What you do with your life
> after the moment of salvation is your gift to God,
> and *that* is what is going to be evaluated
> at the *bema* of Christ.

This phrase "of what sort it is" in the Greek text refers to the *quality* of our works. This will be the focus of the evaluation we're going to experience at the Judgment Seat of Christ — and on the basis of that evaluation, rewards will be given or forfeited.

The Divine Prerequisite for Reward

People rightfully ask, "What is the criteria Jesus will use to determine what kind of reward I receive?" Paul answered that question in verse 14 when he said, "If any man's work *abide* which he hath built thereupon, he shall receive a reward."

If what you have done with your life passes the test of time and *abides*, or *survives*, you will receive a reward. According to Paul's words, we will each be rewarded only for what we did that *abides*.

When I first understood this as a young minister, it totally changed the way I looked at my life. When I realized that simply doing a lot of activities would not bring me a reward, I began to refocus on engaging in the *right* activities — in other words, in what God had assigned *me* to accomplish. My focus today is to build works that will survive for generations, for this is what guarantees fruit that will remain for eternity.

Because I know I will one day stand before Christ to be evaluated and receive my reward, I continually ask myself, *Am I executing God's plan for my life in a haphazard or self-serving manner — or am I striving for excellence and diligently endeavoring to do everything HIS way?*

Quick decisions made without serious prayer and without thinking things through often produce works that don't last very long. Tests come in this life that reveal what we built hastily and without long-term thinking. But when we build carefully and with a long-term perspective, what we build can withstand the fire because it was constructed in the right way and with the right heart motives.

When I realized that simply doing a lot of activities would not bring me a reward, I began to refocus on engaging in the *right* activities — in other words, in what God had assigned *me* to accomplish.

Remember that when you stand before the Judgment Seat of Christ, Jesus will not reward you simply for much activity, but for what you built *correctly* and for that which passes the test of time.

HOLD YOURSELF ACCOUNTABLE — CONDUCT YOUR OWN REVIEW

How you build is how you're going to be evaluated.

This should make all of us look closely at what we are doing and how we are building in every area of our lives, even separate from our discussion about eternity.

What we do now will affect us in the future. How we build now determines how long what we're building is going to last. And it's on *that* basis we're going to be evaluated at the *bema* of Christ. If we build with marble and granite — in other words, if we build our lives according to God's plan so that our works abide — verse 14 says we will receive a reward.

How we build now determines
how long what we're building is going to last.

Through the years, Denise and I have made it a practice to periodically review together what we are building with our lives. We ask ourselves penetrating questions about what we are doing to ensure that it is God-birthed and that it will abide, because *these* are the works for which we will receive a reward. We want to build works that last for God's Kingdom and to do them *His* way — because that is how Jesus will evaluate us.

This type of periodic personal review is a good thing for all of us to do. We shouldn't be afraid to evaluate our lives. It's so important that we conduct a thorough review of our lives with the help of the Holy Spirit. That way we can bring correction where adjustments are needed now rather than to wait for that future day when our lives will be evaluated by Christ.

OUR FUTURE TIME OF RECKONING

How intense is this future evaluation going to be? An answer to that question is found in Matthew 25:14-30, where Jesus gave principles of eternal reckoning as He related the parable of the master who gave talents to his servants and then left for a period of time. As the master returned, he called his servants and asked for an account of what they did with the talents he had given to them. And the Bible tells us in Matthew 25:19 that the master "reckoneth with them" at that time.

This word "reckoned" in Greek is a bookkeeping term that means *to compare accounts.* This word could be used to portray an accountant who is putting together a profit-and-loss statement for his boss. He is examining the books to determine the true financial status of the corporation. This is no surface review; it's a very deep and thorough investigation.

In the context of verse 19, this word means *to compare what was given to what the person actually did with what was given.* It means to evaluate: "Did you do anything with what was placed in your charge? Did it stay the same, or did you increase what was entrusted to you?"

By using this word "reckon," Jesus gave insight on how He will deal with us when we stand before the Judgment Seat of Christ. On that day of reckoning, Christ will look at the "profit-and-loss statement" of our lives to evaluate what He gave us compared to what we did with it.

How did we do with what He told us to do? How did we build our lives? What did we do with the assignments, gifts, and talents He gave to us? And on the basis of what Jesus sees during this time of evaluation, He will designate what kind of reward we should receive.

On that day of reckoning, Christ will look at the "profit-and-loss statement" of our lives to evaluate what He gave us compared to what we did with it.

Again, I want to stress that the Judgment Seat of Christ is not a whipping post or a place of judgment and punishment. It is a place of *evaluation* and *designation* to determine rewards that will be given to believers who have been faithful. The Bible tells us explicitly about five different crowns. There may be more, but five are mentioned.

1. *The crown of incorruption:* This is sometimes called the "incorruptible crown." This crown is referred to in First Corinthians 9:25. The apostle Paul describes it as a crown that will be given to believers who have practiced self-discipline in life and run a successful race of faith.

   > **And every man that striveth for the mastery is temperate in all things. Now they do it to obtain a corruptible crown; but we an incorruptible.**
   >
   > **1 Corinthians 9:25**

2. *The crown of rejoicing:* This crown is referred to in First Thessalonians 2:19. It is often called the "soulwinners' crown." Those who are very active in winning souls are going to receive a crown of rejoicing. As Proverbs 11:30 says, "…He that winneth souls is wise."

   > **For what is our hope, or joy, or crown of rejoicing? Are not even ye in the presence of our Lord Jesus Christ at his coming?**
   >
   > **1 Thessalonians 2:19**

3. *The crown of righteousness:* This crown is referred to in Second Timothy 4:8. It describes a crown that is given to those who are longing for Jesus' appearance and have lived a holy life in anticipation of His coming.

   > **Henceforth there is laid up for me a crown of righteousness, which the Lord, the righteous judge, shall give me at that day: and not to me only, but unto all them also that love His appearing.**
   >
   > **2 Timothy 4:8**

4. *The crown of glory:* This crown is referred to in First Peter 5:4. It's often called the "pastors' crown" because it is a crown that will be given to pastors who have faithfully fed and led their flocks.

> **And when the chief Shepherd shall appear, ye shall receive a crown of glory that fadeth not away.**
>
> **1 Peter 5:4**

5. *The crown of life:* This crown is referred to in James 1:12 and Revelation 2:10. It is often referred to as the "martyrs' crown" because this crown will be given to those who remained faithful, even as they suffered in order to do what God had called them to do, and who committed themselves to finishing their race, regardless of the difficulties they encountered in life.

> **Blessed is the man that endureth temptation: for when he is tried, he shall receive the crown of life, which the Lord hath promised to them that love Him.**
>
> **James 1:12**

> **Fear none of those things which thou shalt suffer: behold, the devil shall cast some of you into prison, that ye may be tried; and ye shall have tribulation ten days: be thou faithful unto death, and I will give thee a crown of life.**
>
> **Revelation 2:10**

These five crowns are literal crowns that Christ is going to place on the heads of those who stand before Him. They represent five kinds of rewards that Jesus will distribute according to what each believer has done with what he or she was given while on earth.

In Second Timothy 4:8, the apostle Paul talked about this holy and profoundly anticipated moment when he will stand before the Judgment Seat of Christ. Paul wrote, "Henceforth there is laid up for me a crown of righteousness, which the Lord, the righteous judge, shall give me at that day: and not to me only, but unto all them also that love His appearing."

Thank God, we who are in Christ will not appear before the Great White Throne Judgment. But we *will* all stand — not crawl, not grovel — before the Judgment Seat of Christ. On that day, rewards will be given to us according to our faithfulness to fulfill God's plan for our lives while on earth. And as we stand there and look Jesus in the eyes, if we have done well, we will hear Him say, "Well done, thou good and faithful servant" (*see* Matthew 25:21).

That thought should thrill your heart if your desire is to live right and please God in all that you do. As I have learned to live more and more thoughtfully and intentionally for Christ over the years, I have come to the place where everything I do is in anticipation of and in preparation for that day when I will stand before Him. I live to hear Jesus say those two simple words to me: *"Well done."*

We have come to the conclusion of our discussion on the fundamental doctrines necessary to build a strong foundation in our Christian walk. Hebrews 6:1,2 ends its list by saying we must know the doctrine of eternal judgment. As we have seen, there will be the Great White Throne Judgment, before which every unbeliever will stand and receive eternal judgment. But for believers, there is a different type of reckoning in the future that involves evaluation and designation rather than judgment and condemnation. Every person who is in Christ will stand before the Judgment Seat of Christ in Heaven and give account for deeds done while in the body, whether good or bad.

As I have learned to live more and more thoughtfully and intentionally for Christ over the years, I have come to the place where everything I do is in anticipation of and preparation for that day when I will stand before Him. I live to hear Jesus say those two simple words to me: *"Well done."*

Once these elementary doctrines are understood and firmly set in place in your life, your spiritual foundation will be strong enough for you to begin pursuing some deeper truths. But without a solid understanding of these six fundamental principles, you're not equipped to go much further.

Within these pages, you have been given Heaven's blueprint for laying a strong spiritual foundation and for reaping the benefits of being a doer of God's Word. Now it's up to you to work with that blueprint and to stay on the path of obedience that leads to your success in every area of life.

Your Eternal Future Will Be Determined by Your Choices on the Earth

What you have read in this chapter about the doctrine of eternal judgment is so important for you to understand, because one day in your future, you will come before the *bema* of Jesus. On that day, you will stand before Him without shame or condemnation as He evaluates your life and bestows your rewards for serving Him with all your heart.

But if you have not yet repented and made Jesus the Savior and Lord of your life, I want to compassionately tell you that unless you do that, there is coming a day in the future when you will be raised to stand before the Great White Throne to be judged for rejecting Jesus. If you die without faith in Christ, the Bible is *absolutely* clear — your future is a lake of fire. There is no negotiating about this truth.

This is why it's so very important that you make a decision for Christ *now*. The "Prayer To Receive Salvation" on page 235 will help you do just that. Not only will that decision save you eternally, but it will also bring deliverance in your present life on earth. With that one decision, you will be empowered to live a life free from the dominion of Satan's kingdom and to fulfill the divine purpose you were born on the earth to accomplish.

And if you are already a child of God, the best way to respond to what you learned in this chapter is to make a decision to conduct your affairs and build your life and your works in a way that *lasts*. Determine today that you will do right, think right, and build right according to the Word of God to the best of your ability all the days of your life. The Holy Spirit within you will help and empower you to follow through on that decision. Then one day, you will stand before Jesus and hear His loving words spoken directly to you: *"Well done, good and faithful servant."*

Determine today that you will do right,
think right, and build right according to
the Word of God to the best of your ability
all the days of your life.

PRAYER TO LAY THE FOUNDATION
OF ETERNAL JUDGMENT

Father, thank You that You strengthen me every step of the way to live my life right. Thank You for the indwelling presence of Your Spirit, who empowers me to stay consistent and committed to building my life correctly on the strong foundation of Your eternal Word. I draw on the Holy Spirit to help me always stay faithful to my responsibility to evaluate my life with His guidance and wisdom so I can hear Jesus' words of commendation as I stand before Him on that day.

I pray for those who don't yet know Jesus as their Savior — that the Holy Spirit would open their eyes and bring them to a saving knowledge of Christ. Thank You for helping me stay alert and willing to seize every opportunity to share the truth of the Gospel that others may escape the Great White Throne Judgment and look forward to a blessed eternity with You. In Jesus' name, amen.

THINK ABOUT IT

You are currently in a qualification period to determine your rank of responsibility in the next age of the Kingdom of God. This is a time for you to conduct your own personal review and self-evaluation while you have time to make necessary adjustments that will make all the difference whether you are ruler over little or a ruler over much in the age to come.

Are you executing God's plan for your life in a haphazard or self-serving manner — or are you striving for excellence and diligently endeavoring to do everything *His* way to prove yourself faithful to Him? What can God trust you to not only step out in faith to *start*, but also to press through in obedience to *finish*? When the Lord examines the "profit-and-loss statement" of your life, will that ledger reveal that you increased and multiplied what He gave you — or that you allowed fear of failure or the unknown to keep you clinging to your status quo?

Think about it: What have you done with the time, talents, opportunities, relationships, and spiritual investments God gave you to utilize in obedience to Him and for His glory? How have you handled the assignments and talents He gave to you? How will you handle them from this day forward? These are His gifts to you. What you do with them is your gift to Him. When you stand before Him, what gift will you be able to lay at His feet?

How you build your life will be evaluated. When you stand before the Judgment Seat of Christ — the *bema* of Christ — your works will be tested with the fire of His holiness. Based on your obedience to His specific plan and instructions and the motivations of your heart with which you carried them out, your works will either emerge as pure gold or be reduced to hay and stubble. If you build your life according to God's plan and ways, your works will abide and you will receive a reward.

How are you living your life? One day you will surely stand before Jesus. He will not shame or humiliate you, but He will address how you ran your race. Will you hear Him say *"Well done"*? Or, will He ask you, *"Well, what have you done?"* That is something to think about.

Your earthly choices determine your eternal future and reward. It's important for you to understand, because one day in your future you will stand before Jesus. If you have repented and received Him as your Savior and Lord, you will meet Him at the *bema*, the Judgment Seat of Christ. He will evaluate your life without doling out shame and condemnation, and bestow rewards upon you for faithfully serving Him. But if you have not yet repented, there is coming a day in the future when you will be raised to stand before the Great White Throne to be judged for rejecting Jesus. If you die without faith in Christ, the Bible is *absolutely* clear — your future is the lake of fire. This is a non-negotiable truth.

So it is vitally important that you make a decision for Christ *now*. This not something for you just to think about — this is a truth you must act upon. Believing and receiving Jesus Christ for who He said He is will not only save you eternally, it will also set you free presently. Aren't you ready to step into the divine purpose you were born to fulfill? Christ is the foundation for you to build upon. And right now is the perfect time.

9

ARE YOU A DISCIPLE
OR A HEARER ONLY?

We've seen how essential the six fundamental doctrines listed in Hebrews 6:1,2 are for us to understand in order to build a strong foundation for our lives in Christ. But it's not just a matter of understanding these "starting point" doctrines. We're supposed to solidify what we've learned in the previous chapters and move on, building on a sure foundation of the basics — the ABCs of our Christian faith. We're not just adding to our reservoir of Bible knowledge so we can accumulate more knowledge of other doctrines. God expects us to commit ourselves to *live* according to the revelation we've gained from Hebrews — to begin to *do* what we have learned. It's both *hearing* and *doing* that establishes the foundation in our lives upon which we can effectively build.

In this chapter, we're going to talk about how to be a doer of the Word we've learned and not a hearer only. And that is the definition of a true disciple or committed learner, — someone who not only understands the elementary doctrines of the faith, but who also makes the decision to remove every wrong belief system, adjust every misguided mindset, and truly embrace those truths until they take root in his life. He is a *doer* of the Word he's hearing, learning, and understanding.

The Art of 'Laying Apart'

Let's focus in on James 1:21-25 and explore what it means to fully receive the Word of God into our lives in a way that actually promotes lasting transformation and an ever-increasing walk of power. We don't want to be hearers only. The Bible *commands* us to be doers.

We are called to lead people into repentance; to make sure they have a faith that is in Christ and Christ alone; and to help people get saved, water baptized, and filled with the Holy Spirit. We are responsible for finding opportunities to lay hands on the sick to see them recover and to impart blessing to people through the laying on of hands as the Holy Spirit leads. We're to encourage believers to live for God on earth so they can experience the joy of their heavenly rewards. Similarly, we're to warn the unsaved that the only eternal recourse for one who rejects Christ is the lake of fire. God has made a way for us to do all of these things, because He included them in His Word as foundational principles that help define our walk with Him. They're important to God, and we have the ability to do them!

James 1:21 provides key instruction to ensure that you are a doer of the Word you have just learned and, thus, a true disciple of Jesus. It says, "Wherefore lay apart all filthiness and superfluity of naughtiness, and receive with meekness the engrafted word, which is able to save your souls." Let's take this verse apart and explore what each part means so you can really understand it.

If you read verse 21 in context, you see that James was talking about our response to the Word of God that we have heard. James wrote, "*Lay apart* all filthiness and superfluity of naughtiness."

The phrase "lay apart" is translated from the compound Greek word *apotithimi*. The word *apo* means *away*, and the word *tithimi* means *to lay down* or *to place*. When you compound the two words, the new word *apotithimi* means *to take something off, to lay it down, and to push it away and put space between you and that object*. This word *apotithimi* paints the picture of *someone making sure a certain object is so far from him that he can't reach it to pick it up and put it back on again*.

In fact, this is the Greek word used to describe *the act of removing old, dirty clothes*. So think about what that's like when you come to the end of the day and it's time for you to go to bed. If you've been wearing dirty clothes, how do you get your clothes off? Do you stand in front of the mirror and say, "Okay, clothes, I'm done with you. You're no longer needed, and you're dirty. I'm finished with you!" — and then expect your clothes to just jump off of your body? Of course not. If that's how you tried to do it, you'd go to bed still wearing your dirty clothes. The only way you're going to get your clothes off your body is by making the decision to utilize your hands, even if you don't explicitly think through the entire process: *"I'm going to push these buttons through the button holes. I'm going to unzip this zipper. I'm going to take my arms out of these sleeves one at a time. I'm going to take off these pants one leg at a time, and I'm going to remove these dirty clothes from my body."*

Now let's apply this analogy to the phrase "lay apart" in James 1:21. James was saying that as we hear the Word of God, we may discover an area of our lives or a belief system that doesn't line up with the Word. When that happens, it isn't enough for us to simply recognize that something isn't right in our walk with God. That isn't going to change us. We have to make a decision *to deliberately remove what is wrong from our lives.*

This is actually describing the act of repentance. Repentance is the conscious decision to embrace God's truth and then make any needed changes to line up with that truth. It is to pray along this line: "Lord, the way I think about and deal with this area of my life is wrong. Therefore, I'm going to begin taking steps right now to get my way of thinking about this in line with Your Word. I'm going to take off that wrong mindset and lay it down." And because the word *apo* is part of that Greek word *apotithimi*, you are actually saying, "I'm going to put so much space between me and that old, sinful mindset that I won't be able to easily reach over, pick it up, and put it back on again!"

That *apo* component is an important one, because when we've thought wrongly about something for a long time, we're very easily inclined to pick up that wrong mindset again, "put it back on," and continue to think that way. We see, then, that James was talking about our responsibility to *make a permanent break* with what the Holy Spirit points out as wrong in our lives — *pushing it so far away from us that we can never reach it again.*

It reminds me of a story I once read of a man who wanted to lose weight but kept going to the refrigerator to look for something tasty that he shouldn't eat. And after eating what he shouldn't have eaten, he would pray again, "Oh, God, please help me change." The man sincerely wanted to change — but his flesh *so* wanted to eat the wrong type of food. Finally, in desperation the man padlocked the refrigerator and put the key in a place he couldn't easily get to. In other words, he did something to prohibit himself from being able to readily open the refrigerator door and violate his diet!

Of course, that man's solution for his particular problem wasn't permanently practical, since eventually he would have to open that refrigerator door and choose the right food to eat. But what he did to his refrigerator door to solve his problem illustrates my point. This is the strategy you have to adopt concerning any area of your life that grieves the Holy Spirit. You must do whatever is necessary to make it very difficult to transgress the commitment you made before God to change in that area.

Perhaps you're giving up cigarettes or another bad habit. Or maybe you know you've been associating with a wrong person or group of people. Or perhaps you have come to realize you have a wrong way of thinking or believing that doesn't line up with God's Word. Whatever it is, you have to do something to permanently bar yourself from going in that wrong direction again. You have to *apotithimi* — take that hindrance off your life, lay it down, and then push it so far away from you that you will never be able to reach for it to put it back on again.

Notice what James said next: "Lay apart all filthiness and superfluity of naughtiness." Taken in context, he was talking about wrong believing and wrong thinking — and in the strongest terms. That word "filthiness" is the Greek word *rhuparia*, which describes *someone or something that is so dirty that he or it stinks.* This word *rhuparia* can also mean *exceptionally cheap* or *low quality.* This means when we walk in the way of sin, it causes us to drastically *devalue* ourselves.

*James was talking about our responsibility
to make a permanent break with what the Holy Spirit
points out as wrong in our lives — pushing it so far
away from us that we can never reach it again.*

Many years ago when Denise and I pastored in Arkansas, there was a mentally challenged man who came to our church, and he just didn't know to practice proper hygiene. When he walked through the door of the building, we knew that he was there because we could smell his entrance! He was grimy; his elbows were dirty; and his clothes stunk. He worked in a chicken factory in the midst of the blood of slaughtered chickens, and he would come to church still dressed in his soiled, blood-stained work clothes! Every time I see this phrase "lay apart all filthiness" from the Greek word *rhuparia*, my thoughts immediately go back to that man.

James used the Greek word *rhuparia* in this verse to make it very clear how the Holy Spirit views the sin we hold on to versus "laying it apart." When we entertain and tolerate a wrong mindset, an erroneous belief, or an unbiblical way of acting in our lives, the Holy Spirit says, *"That sin carries a stench. Spiritually, it is grimy — filthy! Yet you've made the decision to continue in what you're doing, what you're thinking, and what you're believing, even though you know that it's wrong and not fit for your life in Me."*

James went on to further describe this ongoing condition of filthiness by writing "superfluity of naughtiness." The word "superfluity" is a Greek word that describes *a river so swollen with water that it's now spilling out of its banks.* This means if you don't get a grip on what is wrong in your life, it will just continue to get worse and worse and *worse* until it becomes an overspilling *superfluity* and begins to affect every part of your life.

The Bible calls this condition "superfluity of naughtiness." The word "naughtiness" comes from the Greek word *kakia* and depicts *something rank, something foul,* or *something filled with stench.* Whatever is being described with this word is just a horrible, putrid mess!

How does an area of a believer's life sink into this rancid condition? It happens when the Holy Spirit confronts the believer about a spiritually degenerative process in his life, and the believer chooses to remain stuck in his condition, even though he knows that his actions, habits, system of belief, or ways of thinking are wrong. For this type of believer, it just takes too much effort to make the necessary changes. Consequently, his condition becomes spiritually grimy, stinky, and, finally, *putrid.*

If you don't get a grip on what is wrong in your life, it will just continue to get worse and *worse* and worse until it becomes an overspilling *superfluity* and begins to affect every part of your life.

That's what James meant when he wrote, "Wherefore lay apart all filthiness and superfluity of naughtiness, and receive with meekness the engrafted word, which is able to save your souls." He was saying in essence, *"Hey, get rid of that hindrance. Take it off. Lay it down. Get it away from you! Instead of walking around in all that filth, all that wrong thinking, all that wrong believing, receive with meekness the engrafted word, which is able to save your souls."*

A Transplant That Will Save Your Life

Let's look at that phrase in James 1:21, "Receive with meekness the *engrafted* word." The word "engrafted" is the Greek word

213

emphutos, which describes *something that was put in you later on in life* or *something that is subsequently planted in you at a later date.* In other words, you were not born with this; it was not original with you. It is something that was placed *into* you subsequent to your natural birth.

The best illustration of this concept would be an organ transplant. When someone has an organ that has failed, that person's life is in jeopardy unless someone donates his or her organ, allowing the person with a diseased organ to receive an organ transplant. The organ transplanted into the patient's body during that surgery isn't original to that person, but he has to have it in order to live.

It's interesting that when a donor organ is placed in a patient, his or her body immediately tries to reject it. Think about that. The new organ is there — placed inside to save the person. He cannot live without it. But because it's not original in him, his body says, *"This doesn't fit. This isn't comfortable. This was not originally a part of me."* And the only way the transplant surgery will be deemed a success is if the patient's body finally "receives with *meekness*" that "engrafted" organ.

The word *emphutos* that James used when writing about the "engrafted word" carries that same idea. Here we have the picture of someone who has his own ideas about things, his own belief system. Maybe he has grown up in an environment of traditional religious ideas. But then he hears that the Word of God has the power to save his soul — the power to transform him from the inside out. And he makes a decision that he is going to receive the Word with "meekness."

The word "meekness" comes from the Greek word *prautes*, which describes *a person who knows and likes what he thinks, but has decided to lay aside and deny his own feelings, deny his own thoughts, deny his own opinions, and willfully and deliberately submit to the authority of someone else in order to receive what that person has to say or impart to him.* James was saying in this verse that the only way God's Word will ever take root in a person is through this quality of *prautes*, or "meekness."

When people hear the word "meek," they often think that it means someone who is weak. That is not what the Greek word *prautes* means at all. Rather, *prautes* describes someone who thinks he is right but has submitted himself to someone else. He therefore makes the deliberate decision to deny himself the right to act on what he thinks or prefers and to instead submit himself to the word of that person he has committed to serve.

To receive the Word of God with meekness, you have to say "no" to your old ways, "no" to your flesh, and "no" to your own opinions, which are usually very strong. You have to deny yourself, open your heart, and deliberately say, "I am going to receive what I need from the One I have committed my life to."

Five Steps to a Successful 'Transplant' of God's Word in Your Life

In order for the Word of God to be truly transplanted in you, there are five steps you must take:

1. *Submission:* You have to be submitted to the Word and the authority of God. You have to make a decision that you're going to come under God's authority, believe what He says, and do what He tells you to do, regardless of how you feel.

2. *Elimination:* You have to eliminate all other voices, feelings, and opinions — including your own. Eliminate anything that would distract you.

3. *Decision:* You have to make the decision: "I will *not* veer from God's Word. I'm going to be committed to what He says and to the principles of His Word. I'm in this for the long haul!"

4. *Continuation:* You can't just follow these steps once. You have to continually implement them — continually denying yourself, continually remaining in submission to the Word of God, continually eliminating whatever is a hindrance to your spiritual walk. You have to continually say, "I'm going to receive this word. This word may not feel natural to me. It may be different than what I've been taught in the past. However, this is the word that has the power to save me, change me, heal me, and totally alter my entire course of life, and I need to have this if I'm going to live the fullness of what God intends for my life."

5. *Reception:* As you follow steps 1 through 4, things finally kick into gear and the Word begins to produce life in you. You begin to truly receive the Word of God into your life. When you reach this stage of true reception, this verse says the Word "is able to save your soul."

The word "able" in James 1:21 comes from the Greek word *dunamis* and describes *power.* When you deny yourself and open your heart to the Word of God — when you submit to the Word, eliminate wrong thinking, make the decision to stick with the Word, and continue in the Word daily in order to deeply receive from its eternal truths — all of these right decisions release a flood of divine power in you and through you. It's like that transplanted organ when it finally begins to take root and function correctly in the new environment — and, as a result, preserves a life. As you embrace the truths of God's Word, the life in that engrafted Word will begin to release its saving power into your soul.

The word "save" is the Greek word *sozo*. It means *to deliver, to save,* or *to heal.* The word "soul" is the Greek word *psyche* and refers to the *mind* or the *emotions. If you'll embrace the Word and make a decision to submit to it, the Word of God will begin to deliver your head* — and it's your head that needs to be delivered because that's where all the wrong thinking takes place.

The saving power in the Word also works to heal your body, prolong your life, deliver you from bondages of every sort, and cause every area of your life to prosper and be blessed. You *must* have the engrafted Word in order to grow and thrive in this life. Yet when you first hear the Word and its truth enters your heart, your mind may be tempted to reject it.

This is a common occurrence as the engrafting process begins to work in a person's soul. He begins to read the Word or hear the principles of the Word taught, and the Word enters his heart. The spirit of the person is drawn to the life in that truth. Meanwhile, his traditional belief system might be causing him to think thoughts like, *Wait a minute. That isn't what I've heard in the past. I don't know if I like this.*

Soon the person's unrenewed mind begins to try to reject the truth that doesn't fit. Or perhaps this person's flesh doesn't like what the Bible is telling him that he needs to change in his life. So just as the human body tries to reject a donor organ, this person's flesh or mind may try to reject the Word that has been engrafted into his heart with the power to save his soul.

As you embrace the truths of God's Word,
the life in that engrafted Word will begin
to release its saving power into your soul.

What does the medical world do to help a person receive a donor organ that his body will no doubt be tempted to reject? First, the person has to submit to an operation and be willing to have his body opened up in order to exchange his damaged organ for the new one. Then he has to submit to the very tender care of a doctor, who has the responsibility of hovering over him and keeping watch over his condition. The patient also has to faithfully take the prescribed medicine in order to help his body adapt to the donor organ so it can thrive in its new environment. Usually the transplant patient will have to take that medication regularly for the rest of his life, since his body will always be tempted to reject this organ that wasn't originally a part of him. But, finally, that healthy donor organ will begin to kick in and work the way it is supposed to — and as it does, it saves the life of that person.

That's exactly how this soul-saving process of "receiving the engrafted word with meekness" works. And it is exactly what we have to do when the Word of God comes to us. We must follow those five steps that cause us to receive the Word with meekness: *submission, elimination, decision, continuation,* and *reception.* These steps are essential if the engrafted Word is going to begin to produce the power to change us from the inside out and, in the process, save our soul.

Consider what you have learned in the previous chapters on the foundational doctrines that you need to understand. Take, for instance, repentance. You may not like to repent. You may not even feel like repenting. But like it or not, the act of repentance will save your life. You have to choose to submit to and receive what God says about repentance and then do it and continue in it.

> These steps are essential if the engrafted Word is going to begin to produce the power to change us from the inside out and, in the process, save our soul.

Then you must make the decision that you're going to eliminate everything in you that says you don't need to repent. From this point on, you're going to begin to repent whenever you need to because you are submitted to the Word of God. As you continue in that commitment, the truth about repentance and its fruit will kick in, and you'll begin to receive the reward of your obedience. Your willingness to walk with a clean heart before the Lord will release life-transforming power in your life. *It will save your soul.*

SUBMIT TO THE PROCESS OF BECOMING OBEDIENT

James went on to write in verse 22, "Be ye doers of the word, and not hearers only, deceiving your own selves." The Greek that is translated "be ye doers" actually means, *"Be ye becoming."* In other words, you might not immediately know how to do everything in God's Word that is preached to you, but you can start where you are. Sometimes there is a *process* of becoming fully obedient to the Word that you hear.

For example, when Denise and I decided to tithe many years ago, we were in the early years of ministry and we didn't know how we were going to do it. All we had was just a tiny amount of income every month to work with for all our basic needs. We didn't yet understand the principle of tithing, so in our way of thinking, it seemed like we didn't have any money left over to tithe.

At that time, I thought, *If I give ten percent of what we receive in a month, I'm not going to have anything left to buy food to feed our child.* So I didn't jump into tithing with full-fledged obedience in the beginning. I started where I was and built from there. I began doing the Word of God, giving as much toward our tithe as I thought I was able. And as I did, our income began to grow little by little, and as I grew in my conviction of this truth and in my obedience to it, tithing the full amount finally became a determined act of my will. I finally came to the place where I'd received that saving truth wholeheartedly and I wouldn't swerve from it.

Sometimes we have to start where we are and make the decision to be obedient. That's what verse 22 is referring to when it says, "Be ye doers of the word…." As I said earlier, the Greek literally says, *"Be ye becoming."* So if we can't immediately get all the way to the finish line of our obedience in a particular area, we should at least start where we are and determine to do what we are able to do. That decision then *begins* the process of our becoming doers of the Word.

You might not immediately know how to do everything in God's Word that is preached to you, but you can start where you are. Sometimes there is a *process* of becoming fully obedient to the Word that you hear.

The word "doer" is the Greek word *poietes*, which is a word of *creativity*. It's where we get the word for *a poet* — a profession that definitely has a creative flare. The use of this word carries the meaning that if you can't find a way to conveniently obey the Bible in an area, you are to *get creative* and *find* a way. There is *always* a way for you to do what God says.

What Does It Mean To Be a 'Hearer Only'?

Remember, you are called to be a disciple or a committed learner who is listening, learning, and applying what you learn. God doesn't call you to be a hearer only. He calls you to be a *learner* and a *doer*.

But what does it mean to be "hearers only"? We find the answer in the meaning of the Greek word *akroates*, which is translated "hearers only" in James 1:22: "And not hearers only, deceiving your own selves." This word *akroates* was a word used to describe *students who attend a class but aren't serious about learning what the class offers*. They are merely auditing the course.

These are students who just showed up because the rest of the class was there or because it was required for them to be present. But these students didn't really listen or pay attention. They just wanted to make sure that their name was marked as present in class. They were present physically, but *mentally* they weren't really there. They were just hearers only — or you could even say they were just *auditors* or *attenders*.

I think back to the time I attended university. I really applied myself in some of my classes, such as journalism, history, marketing, and advertising. I loved those subjects and could hardly wait to get to class. I wanted not only to hear everything my professor had to say — I also wanted to put what I learned into practice. I had an active desire to be the best I could be in those subjects. In those particular classes, I was truly a disciple.

And then there was my Greek class! I fell in love with the Greek language during my time in the university. I've been studying the Greek language for decades now, but it all started in my university Greek class. I loved my professor, who was such a genius when it came to language. He met with me privately a few times, but that wasn't enough for me. So I scheduled more private sessions with him, and he graciously tutored me one-on-one in the Greek language. I just loved studying Greek and really applied myself — not just to hear or to mark that I was present, but to actually put into practice what I was learning.

But then there were other classes that I did *not* want to apply my efforts toward learning, such as zoology. Oh, I detested that class! I showed up in class only so it would be marked that I was present. I was physically sitting in my zoology class, but mentally I was somewhere else — usually in my Greek or my journalism class. I couldn't have cared less about which animals have vertebrae and which ones don't. It just wasn't interesting to me. I was merely an attender, with no interest in listening and no intention of applying anything about zoology to my life. I was a *hearer only* in that class — which is a good example of the word *akroates* as it is used in James 1:22.

This verse tells us that there are two kinds of Christians. Number one, there is the doer — one who hears the teaching of the Word and diligently finds a way to put what he heard into practice. This is the attribute of a true disciple.

Number two, there is the one who shows up only because he's expected to. He goes to church because that's where all his friends are. He likes the people there; he enjoys the music. But when it comes to the ministry of the Word, this person simply "checks out." He's physically present, but mentally and spiritually, he's not really there. He's just taking up space on the pew or chair. He's not a serious listener; he is an attender — a hearer only. He has no intention of ever doing much of anything with what he's heard — that is, if he ever really heard anything.

Verse 22 concludes by saying, "…deceiving your own selves." This phrase "deceiving your own selves" comes from the Greek word *paralogizomei*, and it means *to make a miscalculation*. It was borrowed from the world of libraries. In libraries, scholars would put documents side by side to compare and analyze the information contained in both documents. If they made a wrong analysis or came to a wrong conclusion, their wrong conclusion was called a *paralogizomei* — translated "deceiving your own selves" in this verse.

James was saying in effect, *"If you think you're going to score great in life and things are going to be better just because you came to church, you have made a tragic miscalculation. Your analysis of your situation is wrong. Just showing up is not going to produce results in your life."*

Of course, showing up is important because it's part of being faithful. But if that Word is going to do anything in you, you have to listen to it *and* find a way to obey it. You have to be a *doer* of the Word. That is what the Bible says.

UNDERSTANDING
YOUR SPIRITUAL STATUS

In James 1:22, James was essentially asking: *"What kind of believer are you? Are you really a disciple doing something with what's being preached? Are you serious about it? Or are you just showing up so it can be marked that you were present?"*

So I want to ask you — are you a doer of the Word, or are you just an "attender"? Christ calls you to be a disciple or a learner who *does* something with what you have heard.

If you have no real intention of doing anything with what you've heard, you are a hearer only — and according to the end of that verse, you are probably deceiving yourself, because it isn't just the hearing of the Word that changes you. It's when you *do* the Word of God that its power is released in you.

To help you honestly locate yourself, let's move on to James 1:23, where James described the person who hears only: "For if any be a hearer of the word, and not a doer, he is like unto a man beholding his natural face in a glass." The word "glass" is really the word for *a mirror*. So this verse pictures a man who looks in the mirror and sees his natural face. The Greek actually could be translated, *"like a man who looks in the mirror at the face he was born with."*

When most of us look in the mirror at the face we were born with, we wish we could trade it for another face. Or we wish we could lose weight. Or we wish that we could have a face lift. Most of us see something about ourselves we don't like. That's the visual James wanted to give us in verse 23.

This verse depicts a man who goes to the mirror and immediately sees what he needs to fix as he is "beholding himself." He sees the face he was born with displaying all its flaws, and it's clear to him that he needs to shave, brush his teeth, and work on his appearance, etc. But rather than give attention to what he sees and take action to make some needed changes, he "...beholdeth himself, and goeth his way, and straightway forgetteth what manner of man he was" (v. 24). In other words, he thinks, *Wow, I need to make a change. Well, one of these days, I'll do that...* Then rather than spend time with the Lord in His Word and in prayer to deal with the flaws he sees, this person delays change and goes on his way.

Are you a doer of the Word, or are you just an "attender"?
Christ calls you to be a disciple or a learner who
does something with what you have heard.

I can use the area of losing weight in my life as an example. I identify with people who struggle with their weight. I know what it's like to stand on the scale and think, *Oh, my, I need to do something about my weight. This is getting worse and worse and worse* — only to hop off that scale and soon be back in the kitchen to eat whatever I wanted to eat once again. In other words, I know what it is to go years not acting on things that I knew needed to change in my life — all the while justifying myself with my good intentions.

Not today, but maybe tomorrow. Maybe next week I'm going to do something about this. But the truth is, throughout the day while I was eating the food and my taste buds were singing with joy about all those tasty, unhealthy carbohydrates, I had already forgotten about the number I saw on the scale that morning. That moment was already in the past. I had moved on and had become totally focused on eating food that was only making my situation worse.

Thank God, that is in my past and I became a doer of the Word in that area of my life! I'm now much lighter and feeling fitter than I have felt for many years.

So let's bring this subject home and talk about how *you* might fit into these two verses. Imagine, for instance, that the Spirit of God has been dealing with you about a wrong attitude you've been harboring. He's telling you to repent and to change, but you never take the needed time in the presence of the Lord to really take care of the issue. You recognize that the Holy Spirit is speaking to your heart about it, and you see that the Bible is in agreement with Him. But life is busy, and you're on your way to the next item on your schedule before you've done anything about getting rid of that wrong attitude that the Spirit of God has convicted you about.

Or maybe there is something that needs to be corrected in your finances. The Holy Spirit has been telling you over and over, *"Fix this. Fix this. Fix this."* And you've kept telling yourself, *It's going to be hard to fix this. I will fix it, but I'm not going to fix it today.* In the meantime, you go on your way, spending more money and making more wrong financial decisions, forgetting what you were convicted about earlier in the day.

This type of pattern can go on and on and be repeated in many areas of your life. It could be that the Holy Spirit or the Word of God is speaking to you about your bad attitude toward another person. Or He might bring up an issue in your marriage or with your children, and you know that you need to repent and make some adjustments. The Holy Spirit is so kind. He'll confront you in love and tell you the real situation. When you look into the mirror of the Word, you'll see what you need to change.

But change is difficult for most people, so they often delude themselves into thinking that their situation isn't as bad as it seems. For example, people who are overweight sometimes don't see themselves the way others see them. The scale and their mirror are telling them that they are overweight, but their answer is to deal with the problem superficially by dressing themselves in a way that doesn't reveal all the bulges. But if they think that solves their issue with overeating or eating the wrong kinds of food, they deceive themselves. The Holy Spirit is trying to change their mindset and their lifestyle in this area in order to prolong their lives. But often people don't stay in His presence long enough to deal with the issue at the root and then begin to take real steps to effect that change.

> The Holy Spirit is so kind. He'll confront you in love and tell you the real situation. When you look into the mirror of the Word, you'll see what you need to change.

That's just one illustration, but that type of scenario is exactly what James is talking about. The Word speaks to a believer and convicts his heart as he hears the Word. The next step is to find ways to *do* what he has just heard — but instead, he decides to go on his way, not stopping to do anything about it. He "straightway forgetteth what manner of man he was." Or he loses his conviction and then forgets what the Holy Spirit said to him. In other words, the Word doesn't really sink in.

Gazing Into 'the Perfect Law of Liberty'

That's what the next verse says: "But whoso looketh into the perfect law of liberty, and continueth therein, he being not a forgetful hearer, but a doer of the work, this man shall be blessed in his deed" (James 1:25). This verse is amazing, so let's look at it more closely.

Up to this point, James was using the illustration of a person who looks at himself in a hand mirror and, seeing an area he needs to work on, decides not to do anything about it. But in verse 25, James presented an analogy that stands in stark contrast to the first. He started out, "But whoso looketh into the perfect law of liberty...." Here we again have the picture of a person who looks at himself in a hand mirror and sees things that need to be corrected. But this person doesn't just rush off without dealing with what needs to change. He is so concerned by what he sees that he goes instead to a big table mirror, where he is able to look at the problem more closely.

In other words, this depicts a man who wants to fix what is wrong. He wants to do what is right. He doesn't want to just recognize the areas of his life that need to change and then run off to focus on other things without dealing with those areas. Instead, this man says, "I'm not moving until I really see this clearly and bring correction to my life!" So he hovers over "the perfect law of liberty" as if it were a large table mirror that accurately reveals both what is right and what needs correction in his reflected image.

This phrase is referring to the Word of God. You see, to a doer of the Word, the Bible is not just something he hears. It's not just a message that is preached. To him, it is *the perfect law of liberty*.

First, it is a law to be *obeyed*. The doer's attitude is, "I live by this Word. I obey this Word. And if I am wrong in some area, I'm going to adapt my life to be in agreement with this Word."

To a doer of the Word, the Bible is not just something he hears. It's not just a message that is preached. To him, it is *the perfect law of liberty*.

Then notice, it is called "the perfect law of *liberty*." The word "liberty" is the same Greek word that describes *a slave who has been emancipated*. This man understands, "If I look into the mirror of the Word of God and see areas in my life that need to change — and then *submit* to the Word and allow it to be a law in my life as I do what it says — then God's Word will emancipate me. It will set me free, because this is not a law of bondage. The eternal truths of His Word will free me like a slave who has been emancipated!"

It Takes Work To Be a Doer

Verse 25 goes on to say, "And continueth therein." The doer *continues* to obey the Word from the moment he recognizes what needs to change. He is determined not to leave the table until that flaw in his life is repented of and permanently fixed. Then it says, "This man shall be *blessed* in his deed." The word "blessed" comes from the Greek word *makarios*, which means *hilarious* or *hilarity*. The doer is going to be so blessed that he can hardly contain himself!

That's what you feel when you get set free from yourself. You get so *blessed* that you are making spiritual progress! You are breaking free from former negative patterns and hindrances that have prevented you from living the life of abundance God always intended for you.

Then notice that the Bible goes on to say this man "shall be blessed in his *deed*." One translation says, "shall be blessed in his *work*." The word "deed," or "work," is a translation of the Greek word *ergon*, which tells us that it takes *work* to be a continual doer of the Word.

It is work to obey the Word of God. It is work to take what you've heard and to find a way to creatively do it. If you think you're going to easily become a doer of the Word as described in James 1:25 with little effort or commitment, then wave farewell to your prospects of success — because it is *not* done easily.

That's why the Greek word for learners or students can also be translated *disciples*. To obey Jesus was going to require *discipline*. It was going to take great effort. It was going to take *work* for those 12 disciples to follow Jesus.

That is also what is going to be required of *you*. However, keep hovering over the Word of God, and make this decision: "I'm not leaving this table mirror — I'm not leaving the perfect law of liberty. I'm going to look into the Word of God until I truly see what it says and allow its truth to illuminate my path. And wherever I come up short, I'm going to submit myself to the Word, and it is going to set me free like a slave who has been emancipated. And then I'm going to find a way to do what the Word of God tells me to do!"

The doer *continues* to obey the Word from the moment
he recognizes what needs to change. He is determined
not to leave the table until that flaw in his life
is repented of and permanently fixed.

So what is the reward of your decision to become a disciple? What do you have to look forward to as you accept the work required to become a doer of the Word? The blessing of obedience is included with God's command to obey (*see* v. 25). James said you will be *blessed* and filled with hilarity and laughter as you faithfully walk out this "supernatural transplant" of the engrafted Word in your life.

Within these pages, you have been given Heaven's blueprint for laying a strong spiritual foundation and for reaping the benefits of being a doer of God's Word. Now it's up to you to work with that blueprint and to stay on the path of obedience that leads to your success in every area of life. As you do, you will reap the inevitable harvest — a life that consistently resounds to the glory of God!

THINK ABOUT IT

The six essential doctrines outlined in Hebrews 6 are vital to our Christian foundation. They are our starting point from which we proceed to lay aside sins and weights that would hinder our progress and growth in God. They provide the direction we need to take action that will align us with God's ways so our lives can represent Him accurately as true disciples are called to do.

Disciples are not just listeners; they are learners who choose to do what they have heard. True disciples not only understand the elementary doctrines of the faith, but they also make the decision to remove every wrong belief system, to adjust every misguided mindset, and to truly embrace those truths until they take root in their lives.

Is there an area of your life that the Holy Spirit has prompted you to make a permanent break with something or someone? Have you taken steps to push it so far away from you that you can never reach it again? What decisions have you made to change and recalibrate your life on an ongoing basis to put distance between yourself and that attitude, that action, or that relationship that the Lord has revealed you must lay aside? Are you ready to be a true disciple and obey His instructions?

Just as a physical body must accept a grafted-in organ transplanted in the place of a non-functioning or diseased organ, so, too, we must receive the engrafted Word of God that is able to change our mindsets and deliver our souls from old desires and ineffective ways of thinking.

Are you embracing the Word of God to be truly transplanted in your own life? Have you committed to the Word of God as the final authority in your life? Have you chosen to ignore all other feelings and inclinations that would distract and draw you in a direction that is contrary to God's ways? Have you made the quality decision that you will remain faithful to the principles of God's Word, regardless of your situations, circumstances, or surroundings? These questions are important for you to answer honestly.

Consistency and continuation release the power of God in your life. Are you willing to make this commitment from the heart and devote yourself to fulfilling it? "God's Word may not feel natural to me. It may be different than what I've been taught in the past. However, this is the Word that has the power to save me, change me, heal me, and totally alter my entire course of life. Therefore, I choose to accept and act on this Word so that I can live the fullness of what God intends for my life."

Transformation is a process. And that process starts with the decision to apply effort to change or to do what God requires. Being a doer of the Word is not merely going through the motions of what the Lord instructs. A doer of the Word is one who positions his or her heart not only to understand the will of the Lord, but also to walk in His ways.

In John 14:21 (*AMPC*), Jesus said: "The person who has my commands and keeps them is the one who [really] loves Me...."

This statement from the Master lets us know He views obedience to His words as an expression of love for Him. Therefore, the one who willingly aligns himself to obey God's words will also grow in conformity to His ways.

Does your love for God stimulate a heartfelt desire within you to be like Him? How do you line up when you lay your ways alongside the template of God's Word? Does the fruit of your life announce you as a doer of God's Word or a hearer only? That is something to think about.

PRAYER TO RECEIVE SALVATION

When Jesus Christ comes into your life, you are immediately set free from slavery to sin! If you have never received Jesus as your personal Savior, it is time to experience this new life for yourself. The first step to freedom is simple. Just pray this prayer out loud from your heart:

> Lord, I can never adequately thank You for all You did for me on the Cross. I am so undeserving, Jesus, but You came and gave Your life for me anyway. I repent for rejecting You, and I turn away from my life of rebellion and sin right now. I turn to You and receive You as my Savior, and I ask You to wash away my sin and make me completely new in You by Your precious blood.
>
> I thank You from the depths of my heart for doing what no one else could do for me. Had it not been for Your willingness to lay down Your life for me, I would be eternally lost. Thank You, Jesus, that I am now redeemed by Your blood. On the Cross, You bore my sin, my sickness, my pain, my lack of peace, and my suffering. Your blood has removed my sin, washed me whiter than snow, and given me right-standing with the Father. I have no need to be ashamed of my past sins because I am now a new creature in You. Old things have passed away, and all things have become new because I am in Jesus Christ (*see* 2 Corinthians 5:17).
>
> Because of You, Jesus, today I am forgiven; I am filled with peace; and I am a joint-heir with You! Satan no longer has a right to lay any claim on me. From a grateful heart, I will faithfully serve You the rest of my days! I pray this in Jesus' name, amen!

If you prayed this prayer from your heart, something marvelous just happened to you. No longer a servant to sin, you are now a servant of Almighty God. The evil spirits that once exacted every ounce of your being and required your all-inclusive servitude no longer possess the authorization to control you or dictate your destiny!

As a result of your decision to turn your life over to Jesus Christ, your eternal home has been decided forever. Heaven will now be your permanent address for all eternity.

God's Spirit has moved into your own human spirit, and you have become the "temple of God" (*see* 1 Corinthians 6:19). What a miracle! To think that God, by His Spirit, now lives inside you!

Now you have a new Lord and Master, and His name is Jesus. From this moment on, the Spirit of God will work in you and supernaturally energize you to fulfill God's will for your life. Everything will change for you as you yield to His leadership in your life — and it's all going to change for the best!

Prayer To Receive the Baptism in the Holy Spirit

The baptism in the Holy Spirit is a free gift to *everyone* who has made Jesus Savior and Lord of his or her life (*see* Acts 2:38,39).

After you made Jesus your Lord at the time of the new birth, the Holy Spirit came to live inside you, and your old, unregenerate spirit was made completely new. This subsequent gift is the "baptism into," or *an immersion in*, the Holy Spirit.

The baptism in the Holy Spirit supplies the supernatural power of God for witnessing about Christ, for enjoying a deeper, more intimate relationship with the Holy Spirit, and for victorious Christian living.

Receiving this precious gift is easy. Before you pray to receive the infilling of the Holy Spirit, you might want to read and meditate on the Scripture references I provide at the end of this prayer. Then expect to receive what you ask for *the moment* you pray!

If you would like to be baptized in the Holy Spirit and speak with new tongues (*see* Acts 2:4), simply pray the following prayer and then act on it!

Lord, You gave the Holy Spirit to Your Church to help us fulfill the Great Commission. I ask You in faith for this free gift, and I receive right now the baptism in the Holy Spirit. I believe that You hear me as I pray, and I thank You for baptizing me in the Holy Spirit with the evidence of speaking with a new, supernatural prayer language. In Jesus' name, amen.

As a result of praying this prayer, *your life will never be the same.* You will grow in operating in the gifts of the Holy Spirit. You will learn to experience Jesus' victory as a living reality every day.

Scripture References for Study and Review: Mark 16:17; Luke 24:49; Acts 1:4,5,8; 2:4,39; 10:45,46

About the Author

RICK RENNER is a highly respected Bible teacher and leader in the international Christian community. Rick is the author of a long list of books, including the bestsellers *Dressed To Kill* and *Sparkling Gems From the Greek 1* and *2*, which have sold millions of copies in multiple languages worldwide. Rick's understanding of the Greek language and biblical history opens up the Scriptures in a unique way that enables readers to gain wisdom and insight while learning something brand new from the Word of God.

Rick is the founding pastor of the Moscow Good News Church. He also founded Media Mir, the first Christian television network in the former USSR that broadcasts the Gospel to countless Russian-speaking viewers around the world via multiple satellites and the Internet. He is the founder and president of RENNER Ministries, based in Tulsa, Oklahoma, and host to his TV program that is seen around the world in multiple languages. Rick leads this amazing work with his wife and lifelong ministry partner, Denise, along with the help of their sons and committed leadership team.

CONTACT RENNER MINISTRIES

For further information
about RENNER Ministries,
please contact the office nearest you,
or visit the ministry website at:
www.renner.org

ALL USA CORRESPONDENCE:
RENNER Ministries
P. O. Box 702040
Tulsa, OK 74170-2040
(918) 496-3213
Or 1-800-RICK-593
Email: renner@renner.org
Website: www.renner.org

MOSCOW OFFICE:
RENNER Ministries
P. O. Box 789
101000, Moscow, Russia
+7 (495) 727-1470
Email: blagayavestonline@ignc.org
Website: www.ignc.org

RIGA OFFICE:
RENNER Ministries
Unijas 99
Riga LV-1084, Latvia
+371 67802150
Email: info@goodnews.lv

KIEV OFFICE:
RENNER Ministries
P. O. Box 300
01001, Kiev, Ukraine
+38 (044) 451-8315
Email: blagayavestonline@ignc.org

OXFORD OFFICE:
RENNER Ministries
Box 7, 266 Banbury Road
Oxford OX2 7DL, England
+44 1865 521024
Email: europe@renner.org

Books by Rick Renner

Build Your Foundation*
Chosen by God*
Dream Thieves*
Dressed To Kill*
The Holy Spirit and You*
How To Keep Your Head on Straight in a World Gone Crazy*
How To Receive Answers From Heaven!*
Insights to Successful Leadership*
Last-Days Survival Guide
Life in the Combat Zone*
A Life Ablaze*
A Light in Darkness, Volume One,
   Seven Messages to the Seven Churches series
The Love Test*
No Room for Compromise, Volume Two,
   Seven Messages to the Seven Churches series
Paid in Full*
The Point of No Return*
Repentance*
Signs You'll See Just Before Jesus Comes*
Sparkling Gems From the Greek Daily Devotional 1*
Sparkling Gems From the Greek Daily Devotional 2*
Spiritual Weapons To Defeat the Enemy*
Ten Guidelines To Help You Achieve
   Your Long-Awaited Promotion!*
Testing the Supernatural
Turn Your God-Given Dreams Into Reality*
Why We Need the Gifts of the Spirit*
The Will of God — The Key to Your Success*
You Can Get Over It*

*Digital version available for Kindle, Nook, and iBook.
Note: Books by Rick Renner are available for purchase at:
www.renner.org

SPARKLING GEMS FROM THE GREEK 1

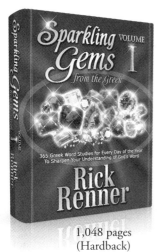

In 2003, Rick Renner's *Sparkling Gems From the Greek 1* quickly gained widespread recognition for its unique illumination of the New Testament through more than 1,000 Greek word studies in a 365-day devotional format. Today *Sparkling Gems 1* remains a beloved resource that has spiritually strengthened believers worldwide. As many have testified, the wealth of truths within its pages never grows old. Year after year, *Sparkling Gems 1* continues to deepen readers' understanding of the Bible.

1,048 pages
(Hardback)

To order, visit us online at: **www.renner.org**

SPARKLING GEMS FROM THE GREEK 2

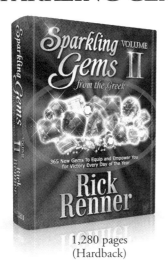

Rick infuses into *Sparkling Gems From the Greek 2* the added strength and richness of many more years of his own personal study and growth in God — expanding this devotional series to impact the reader's heart on a deeper level than ever before. This remarkable study tool helps unlock new hidden treasures from God's Word that will draw readers into an ever more passionate pursuit of Him.

1,280 pages
(Hardback)

To order, visit us online at: **www.renner.org**

DRESSED TO KILL
A Biblical Approach
to Spiritual Warfare and Armor

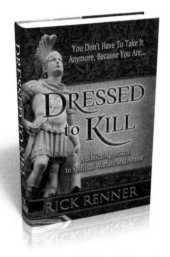

Rick Renner's book *Dressed To Kill* is considered by many to be a true classic on the subject of spiritual warfare. The original version, which sold more than 400,000 copies, is a curriculum staple in Bible schools worldwide. In this beautiful volume, you will find:

- 504 pages of reedited text in paperback

- 16 pages of full-color illustrations

- Questions at the end of each chapter to guide you into deeper study

In *Dressed To Kill*, Rick explains with exacting detail the purpose and function of each piece of Roman armor. In the process, he describes the significance of our *spiritual* armor not only to withstand the onslaughts of the enemy, but also to overturn the tendencies of the carnal mind. Furthermore, Rick delivers a clear, scriptural presentation on the biblical definition of spiritual warfare — what it is and what it is not.

When you walk with God in deliberate, continual fellowship, He will enrobe you with Himself. Armed with the knowledge of who you are in Him, you will be dressed and dangerous to the works of darkness, unflinching in the face of conflict, and fully equipped to take the offensive and gain mastery over any opposition from your spiritual foe. You don't have to accept defeat anymore once you are *dressed to kill*!

To order, visit us online at: **www.renner.org**

Book Resellers: Contact Harrison House at 800-722-6774 or visit **www.HarrisonHouse.com** for quantity discounts.

HOW TO KEEP YOUR HEAD ON STRAIGHT IN A WORLD GONE CRAZY

DEVELOPING DISCERNMENT FOR THESE LAST DAYS

400 pages
(Paperback)

The world is changing. In fact, it's more than changing — it has *gone crazy*.

We are living in a world where faith is questioned and sin is welcomed — where people seem to have lost their minds about what is right and wrong. It seems truth has been turned *upside down*.

In Rick Renner's book ***How To Keep Your Head on Straight in a World Gone Crazy***, he reveals the disastrous consequences of a society in spiritual and moral collapse. In this book, you'll discover what Christians need to be doing to stay out of the chaos and remain anchored to truth. You'll learn how to stay sensitive to the Holy Spirit, how to discern right and wrong teaching, how to be grounded in prayer, and how to be spiritually prepared for living in victory in these last days.

Leading ministers from around the world are calling this book essential for every believer. Topics include:

- Contending for the faith in the last days
- How to pray for leaders who are in error
- How to judge if a teaching is good or bad
- Seducing spirits and doctrines of demons
- How to be a good minister of Jesus Christ

To order, visit us online at: **www.renner.org**

Book Resellers: Contact Harrison House at 800-722-6774 or visit **www.HarrisonHouse.com** for quantity discounts.

LAST-DAYS SURVIVAL GUIDE

A Scriptural Handbook
To Prepare You for These Perilous Times

472 pages
(Paperback)

In his book *Last-Days Survival Guide*, Rick Renner thoroughly expands on Second Timothy 3 concerning the last-days signs to expect in society as one age draws to a close before another age begins.

Rick also thoroughly explains how not to just *survive* the times, but to *thrive* in their midst. God wants you as a believer to be equipped — *outfitted* — to withstand end-time storms, to navigate wind-tossed seas, and to sail with His grace and power to fulfill your divine destiny on earth!

If you're concerned about what you're witnessing in society today — and even in certain sectors of the Church — the answers you need in order to keep your gaze focused on Christ and maintain your victory are in this book!

To order, visit us online at: **www.renner.org**

Book Resellers: Contact Harrison House at 800-722-6774 or visit **www.HarrisonHouse.com** for quantity discounts.

Connect with us on

f Facebook @ **HarrisonHousePublishers**

and Instagram @ **HarrisonHousePublishing**

so you can stay up to date with news

about our books and our authors.

Visit us at **www.harrisonhouse.com**

for a complete product listing as well as

monthly specials for wholesale distribution.

The Harrison House Vision

Proclaiming the truth and the power
of the Gospel of Jesus Christ with excellence.
Challenging Christians
to live victoriously,
grow spiritually,
know God intimately.